T0068182

There's Always More to Every Story

Donald Marshall

WESTBOW
PRESS®
A DIVISION OF THOMAS NELSON
& ZONDERVAN

Copyright © 2022 Donald Marshall.

All rights reserved. No part of this book may be used or reproduced by any means, graphic, electronic, or mechanical, including photocopying, recording, taping or by any information storage retrieval system without the written permission of the author except in the case of brief quotations embodied in critical articles and reviews.

This book is a work of non-fiction. Unless otherwise noted, the author and the publisher make no explicit guarantees as to the accuracy of the information contained in this book and in some cases, names of people and places have been altered to protect their privacy.

WestBow Press books may be ordered through booksellers or by contacting:

WestBow Press
A Division of Thomas Nelson & Zondervan
1663 Liberty Drive
Bloomington, IN 47403
www.westbowpress.com
844-714-3454

Because of the dynamic nature of the Internet, any web addresses or links contained in this book may have changed since publication and may no longer be valid. The views expressed in this work are solely those of the author and do not necessarily reflect the views of the publisher, and the publisher hereby disclaims any responsibility for them.

Any people depicted in stock imagery provided by Getty Images are models, and such images are being used for illustrative purposes only. Certain stock imagery © Getty Images.

Cover Design by Jacey Johnson

ISBN: 978-1-6642-5099-4 (sc)
ISBN: 978-1-6642-5101-4 (hc)
ISBN: 978-1-6642-5100-7 (e)

Library of Congress Control Number: 2021924047

Print information available on the last page.

WestBow Press rev. date: 02/16/2022

NIV: Scripture quotations taken from The Holy Bible, New International Version® NIV® Copyright © 1973 1978 1984 2011 by Biblica, Inc. TM. Used by permission. All rights reserved worldwide.

NKJV: Scripture taken from the New King James Version® Copyright © 1982 by Thomas Nelson. Used by permission. All rights reserved.

ESV: "Scripture quotations are from the ESV® Bible (The Holy Bible, English Standard Version®), copyright © 2001 by Crossway, a publishing ministry of Good News Publishers. Used by permission. All rights reserved."

NLT: Scripture quotations marked (NLT) are taken from the Holy Bible, New Living Translation, copyright ©1996, 2004, 2015 by Tyndale House Foundation. Used by permission of Tyndale House Publishers, a Division of Tyndale House Ministries, Carol Stream, Illinois 60188. All rights reserved.

BSB: The Holy Bible, Berean Study Bible, BSB Copyright ©2016, 2018 by Bible Hub Used by Permission. All Rights Reserved Worldwide.

KJV: Scripture taken from the King James Version of the Bible.

NASB: "Scripture quotations taken from the (NASB®) New American Standard Bible®, Copyright © 1960, 1971, 1977, 1995, 2020 by The Lockman Foundation. Used by permission. All rights reserved. www.lockman.org"

MSG: Scripture taken from The Message. Copyright © 1993, 1994, 1995, 1996, 2000, 2001, 2002. Used by permission of NavPress Publishing Group.

ISV: Scripture taken from the Holy Bible: International Standard Version®. Copyright © 1996-forever by The ISV Foundation. ALL RIGHTS RESERVED INTERNATIONALLY. Used by permission.

Voice: Scripture taken from The Voice™. Copyright © 2012 by Ecclesia Bible Society. Used by permission. All rights reserved.

CEV: Scripture taken from the Contemporary English Version © 1991, 1992, 1995 by American Bible Society. Used by Permission.

GNT: Scripture quotations marked (GNT) are from the Good News Translation in Today's English Version- Second Edition Copyright © 1992 by American Bible Society. Used by Permission.

AMP: Scripture taken from the Amplified Bible, Copyright © 1954, 1958, 1962, 1964, 1965, 1987 by The Lockman Foundation. Used with permission.

GW: Scripture is taken from GOD'S WORD®, © 1995 God's Word to the Nations. Used by permission of Baker Publishing Group.

Contents

Introduction

Paul Harvey's radio broadcast known as *The Rest of the Story* fascinated me from the moment I first heard it. It dealt with history but was never dull, required you to make connections that were seldom obvious, challenged you to beat Mr. Harvey to the punch, and demonstrated that truth is often stranger than fiction and that people's lives and the situations they face are far more complex and filled with twists and turns than we commonly realize. Over thirty years ago I was moved to write a series of nine stories using the format of *The Rest of the Story*. And for these stories I had chosen to look exclusively to the *Bible* and Christianity for ideas, and to God as my source of inspiration.

I shared those stories at a church family camp and in a few other contexts, then forgot about them. Years later I tried to relocate them, even having my very first computer rebuilt so I could extract them from its hard drive. But alas, they weren't there! I had already searched through stacks of papers I had preserved over the years, but with no success.

There was really nothing I could do but start that search over again, and this time I succeeded! This was around the 1st of March, 2020–the beginning of the COVID-19 pandemic. With the free time accompanying forced isolation, I decided to see if I could come up with some more stories featuring a biblically focused theme. A year or so later there were fifty-two total stories, one for each week of the year.

With encouragement from my family, I decided to look into publishing the result, and this is it. Since family and friends seemed to enjoy the stories so much, I am hoping that others will benefit from reading them as well.

Confirming that these are true stories requires careful research and is subject to several difficulties. Not all sources are in agreement, and in many cases there are answers we simply don't know. On the other hand, continuing research may reveal new insights and call for further revision. Given these and other possibilities, I have made every effort to tell the truth.

Special thanks are deserved by Carol, my wife of over fifty-five years, the personnel at WestBow Press who engineered the final product, and Jesus Who loves me and led me along the path.

These stories are meant to inform, entertain, and plant seeds. May our Savior use them to His glory!

A Whale of a Tale

Even in light of the latest scientific efforts to produce more seaworthy ships, more precise and dependable methods of navigation, and more sophisticated search and rescue capabilities, those who ply the seas, who undertake ocean voyages, always incur an element of risk. Imagine how much greater that risk must have been in ages past. Among those in any age who have found themselves cast overboard and left for dead–well, few have ever lived to tell the tale. And when that tale turns out sounding like a fish story, who can blame a person for having their doubts about it.

But then it has often been said that truth is stranger than fiction. And our hero–we'll call him J.–would certainly have agreed with that. You see, J. had a whale of a tale to tell. He had gone to sea, fleeing in the face of one awkward situation, only to find himself in another: the vessel he was in was breaking up beneath him and his fellow voyagers! What followed was a series of events so astounding that many find it difficult to believe they could have ever occurred. Thrown out of the vessel, J. found himself staring into the open mouth of a giant sea monster. Shock and fear coalesced into a piercing scream which was instantly muffled as huge jaws closed around him. He gasped desperately for breath and thrashed wildly about, then, according to the record, fell into a dead faint as waves of muscular contractions projected him into the creature's stomach.[1]

Of course, the story did not end there. J. was miraculously released from the belly of his host, having approached the very gates of death. It is distressing to visualize what his body must have looked like, bleached white by the powerful digestive juices of his giant captor.[2] His appearance would have certainly aroused the curiosity of all who saw him, and he would have no end of opportunities to tell his tale over and over again.

If this event had occurred during the 1980s–the era during which this story is being written–scientists and medical personnel would have come from all over to verify the remarkable incident for themselves. *Life* magazine would have run an exclusive series. J. would have appeared on all the talk shows and on *That's Incredible*, *Ripley's Believe It or Not*, and perhaps even *The Lives of the Rich and Famous*, and his life would have been the subject of a big-budget Hollywood epic!

But there has always been speculation over the tale of Jonah. Some people simply pass it off as a myth. Large marine creatures don't have throats big enough to accommodate a man, and even if they did their stomach acids would be so toxic they would cause rapid death–or so such people say.[3] On the other hand, those people who take the story of Jonah quite literally offer a variety of explanations as to the identity of Jonah's captor. (For Seattle readers: It would certainly have offered fishing from the window if it had had one!) Some are inclined to assume that God did in fact create a special creature just for the occasion. Others suspect that it was a type of animal still present in the ocean today.

The blue whale is the largest creature that's ever lived, reaching lengths of over one hundred feet and having a mouth easily admitting several men. But as a plankton feeder, its esophagus is simply too narrow to allow a human swallowee to pass any farther. However, toothed whales such as the sperm whale and orca (killer whale) could accommodate a human.[4] And the infamous great white shark is not only known for its man-eating reputation, but also its uncanny ability to store food undigested in its stomach for many days.[5] But whatever the case may be, the story of Jonah is a different story altogether.

For the J. of our story was James, not Jonah–James Bartley–a British sailor who in 1891 was swallowed by a sperm whale after its death throes destroyed a longboat from which it had been harpooned. Bartley was retrieved over fifteen hours later when strange movements of the whale's stomach were discovered during the butchering process. Bartley remained unconscious for two weeks but eventually recovered, never to return to sea again. He became a shoe cobbler in his native town of Gloucester, England, and when he died, his tombstone bore the inscription, "James Bartley, a Modern Jonah."[6]

But of course, the story of the biblical Jonah does *not* require that a marine creature which exists today can swallow a man and allow him to survive for days in its stomach. Our Creator both *supernaturally* maintains the order of the physical world and *supernaturally* acts outside of physical limitations, using *both* processes to accomplish His will. The latter process is known as a miracle, and it was the *miracles* of Jesus that authenticated His divine authority (Acts 2:22–24). And a closer reading of the book of Jonah reveals that "the LORD had prepared a great fish to swallow Jonah" (Jonah 1:17 NKJV). Miracles don't call for a "natural" explanation.

And as it turns out, the story of James Bartley's amazing encounter with a whale had been widely circulated for almost one hundred years, when, in 1991, Messiah College Professor Edward B. Davis decided to research the tale. After exhaustive investigation he concluded that it was nothing more than a "fish story" after all! And it seems that its widespread acceptance was at least in part due to a desire on the part of many Christians to employ it to support the validity of *Scripture*.[7] Yes, THERE'S ALWAYS MORE TO EVERY STORY.

All the Starry Host

In the *Bible's* creation account, the primal earth first appears in a dark void into which God introduces electromagnetic radiation–light. Light emanates from energy sources in two forms: those which are visible to the human eye and those, such as infrared and ultraviolet, which are not. The most powerful of these energy sources are the stars, including our sun.[8] And stars are referred to both literally and figuratively in the *Scriptures*. Among these references, consider the following three:

- as countless as the stars in the sky and as measureless as the sand on the seashore (Jeremiah 33:22 NIV)
- while the morning stars sang together (Job 38:7 NIV)
- star differs from star in splendor (I Corinthians 15:41 NIV)

Under ideal conditions, and depending on the clarity of one's vision, somewhere between 5000 and 10,000 stars are visible to the unaided eye. Only half this many can be seen from any one location on earth.[9] And until the invention of the telescope, we had no way of observing any more. Today's more sophisticated optical and radio telescopes have shown that the number of stars is beyond our wildest imagination. There are at least an estimated one hundred thousand million stars in our galaxy,[10] and the observable universe is estimated to contain a minimum of two trillion galaxies![11] But since starlight travels away from a star at a speed of about 670,616,629 mph, stars which may exist beyond the distance over which their[12] light must travel to reach Earth have never yet been seen. Incidentally, estimates of the total number of stars in the visible universe are of the same order of magnitude as the number of grains of sand on earth!

Furthermore, scientists claim that the vast majority of stars were formed early in the history of the universe as masses of dust and gas within a galaxy collapsed under gravitational attraction, causing their cores to heat up until nuclear fusion occurred. All stars emit light as a result of the nuclear fusion of hydrogen atoms into helium.[13]

And because they are not completely solid and are constantly generating waves of energy, stars produce *sound* as well as light. Although these sounds cannot travel through the vacuum of space, they can very slightly alter the brightness of light produced by a star. Because our atmosphere makes it difficult for earth-bound telescopes to detect these subtle changes, scientists depend on telescopes which have been launched into space to detect and measure them. They can then convert them to sounds which we can hear. These sounds vary from star to star, resulting in a symphony-like blend of stellar harmony.[14]

In addition, stars other than the sun are so distant from Earth that even through a telescope they appear as mere pinpoints of light! Most appear white, although they vary in brightness, and they maintain their relative positions as they move across the sky. Until recently little else was known about them. Scientists now believe that each star goes through a life cycle, so that during the stages of their lifetime, stars vary from each other in brightness, color, size, and other ways as well. And at an estimated age of only 13.8 billion years, the universe is apparently not, and may never be, old enough for any stars to have "burned out" completely.[15]

As scientists continue to probe the starry host, their development, structure, energy output, and interactions continue to lend themselves to scientific analysis since humans–God's image bearers–are privileged to think God's thoughts after Him. Certainly those who first heard or read the *Bible's* references to the stars which were quoted above did not perceive their full implications: that the number of stars is vast, that stars sing, and that star differs from star in splendor. But the One who created the stars certainly did! Yes, THERE'S ALWAYS MORE TO EVERY STORY.

Appearances Can Be Deceptive

Dramas require us to willingly *suspend disbelief*, which is often easier if we are unaware of an actor's real-life story. For example, knowing that an actor is a scoundrel can influence our ability to enjoy their role as a model of integrity. However, if we do willingly suspend disbelief, it is possible that we may allow ourselves to be deceived by a drama's version of reality. Magic, on the other hand, seeks to *compel belief*, regardless of a magician's real-life story. If we do believe—even though we are aware of the truth—we have allowed ourselves to be deceived into believing a "lie," just as the magician had intended.

Actually, the word "magic" is derived from the ancient Greek word for a Medo-Persian tribe which practiced Zoroastrianism, a religion that's been around for as many as three thousand years. Based on the teachings of a Persian mystic named Zoroaster, Zoroastrianism incorporates some beliefs that are reminiscent of biblical doctrines: "[I]t exalts an uncreated and benevolent deity . . . as its supreme being, [is] centered on a dualistic cosmology of good and evil and an eschatology predicting the ultimate conquest of evil, [and includes] features . . . such as messianism, judgment after death, heaven and hell, and free will."[16] But at the same time, it leaves out the incarnation and the cross, and incorporates a hodgepodge of ideas that are distinctly non-Christian.[17]

In his book *Thus Spake Zarathustra*, completed in 1895, German philosopher Friedrich Nietzsche unveiled his "God is Dead" concept, which proposed that without a universal moral compass, man would lose the conviction that life had meaning (nihilism)–unless–unless there arose *übermenschen*, a race of supermen with the "creative powers . . . to overcome cultural and moral mores in pursuit of new values and aesthetic health."[18] Nietzsche saw Zarathustra (another spelling of Zoroaster) as the originator of what later became Judeo-Christian morals, and therefore as a worthy *opponent* in Nietzsche's efforts to eliminate what was heeding human progress: belief in God.[19]

Twenty-one years later, Richard Strauss composed "Thus Spake Zarathustra" as a musical tribute to Nietzsche's novel of the same name. The opening fanfare of this orchestral piece, "Sunrise," is considered by many to be the most compelling musical depiction of that daily rebirth ever composed.[20] Elvis Presley used it to set the stage for many of his performances, and its use at the beginning of the sci-fi movie "2001: A Space Odyssey" familiarized it to many of us.[21] All in all, the writings of Nietzsche and this composition by Strauss have, like magic, been devised to *compel belief in a lie* by attempting to make the impossible–that biblical revelation is faulty–appear real.

Of course, Judeo-Christian morality *did not* originate with Zoroaster/Zarathustra, *nor could it ever* be replaced, as Nietzsche would have us believe, by means of the creative powers of an evolved race of supermen with the "will to power . . . the summary of [every] man's struggle against his surrounding environment as well as his reason for living in it."[22] Not even if the attempt is emotionally rationalized by a glorious piece of classical music!

Judeo-Christian morality is not a humanly devised set of propositions but the expression of the character and holiness of the infinite-personal God in the lives of mortal men and women. Efforts to kill God have been remarkably ineffective, with one notable exception. And what Satan and men devised as the "final solution"– nailing Jesus to the cross–sealed the destiny of those who pridefully sought to free themselves from accountability to God. "But to all who did receive him, who believed in his name," who were willing to acknowledge their Creator and humble themselves before Him, "he gave the right to become children of God" (John 1:12 ESV).

Advent and Christmas celebrate the coming of God to earth as a lowly human being in the ultimate revelation of His nature and purpose. Twelve days after Christmas, *Epiphany* (from the Greek word meaning "appearance" or "manifestation), celebrates the first recorded encounter of the baby Jesus with Gentiles–the visitors from the East who have come to worship Him. Epiphany also celebrates the baptism of Jesus years later by John the Baptist when the voice from heaven confirmed that Jesus is both "fully man and fully God."[23] By the way, there is no evidence to substantiate the claim that the song "The 12 Days of Christmas" contains a coded biblical meaning.[24]

As for those visitors from the East, they had witnessed the appearance of "his star" and realized that a "King of the Jews" *who deserved their worship* had been born. Some theologians believe that "His star" was in fact the Shekinah, the light of God's divine glory such as manifested in the pillar of fire which led Israel at night when they left Egypt and traveled through the wilderness.[25] In any case, "His star" led them to the house in which Joseph, Mary, and baby Jesus were then staying. These visitors bowed down to worship Him and presented Him gifts of gold, frankincense, and myrrh. And they were warned by God in a dream to return home another way because King Herod, who would brook no rivals, had deceived them. (Matthew 2:1-12 NIV)

What their names were, whether or not there were three of them, and how many were in their traveling party is unclear. But they were apparently *not* king*s* and were quite probably from some area of present-day Western Iran, then part of the mighty Persian Empire. They were identified as magi or magoi, the Greek word usually referring to Zoroastrian priests, but also the root of the terms "magic and magicians." Magi were noted for their expertise in astronomy, astrology, and other areas of knowledge.[26]

Whoever these particular magi were, it must be that by the

time Jesus' birth approached, God had corrected certain religious misconceptions they had held and assigned them a very special task! These magicians were not out to deceive, but to see for themselves that the promised Messiah had arrived. And subsequently they became the first known Gentiles to spread the good news beyond the borders of Israel! Yes, THERE'S ALWAYS MORE TO EVERY STORY!

Bad Things Happen to Good People

+ + + + + +

In the rural county that I know best, the most commonly held religious belief is that good people go to heaven and bad people go to the other place. At the same time, these country folk are well aware that even good people must deal with bad situations caused by the forces of nature *and* human choices. In other words, *all* people experience bad things. Of course, no one claims to be completely good, nor believes that anyone is completely bad. So, "good" and "bad," as used by these folks, must be relative terms: some good things are better than others, while some bad things are worse than others. Thus it is commonly held that if a person's good deeds outweigh their bad, they are qualified for heaven.

But there are several major problems with this line of thinking. Whose definitions of good and bad are being used? If they are those in the *Bible*, what about statements such as:

> 'Why do you call me good?' Jesus answered. 'No one is good—except God alone' (Mark 10:18 NIV); 'no one does good, not even one' (Romans 3:12 ESV); and 'Whoever breaks one commandment is guilty of breaking them all' (James 2:10 GNT).

Goodness, according to the *Bible*, is the character and holiness of God; no one is good unless they reflect God's goodness in *every*

11

respect! In other words, goodness is the complete absence of badness. If that is so, then we are all less than good. We are in fact bad. Not necessarily as bad as we *could* be, but definitely not as good as we *need* to be.

Christians are convinced (1) that Jesus willingly took the rap for all of our badness in order that His goodness could be justly transferred to us and we can be forgiven, and (2) that thereafter God would recreate us in the image of His Son. But how can God convince non-Christians of their need and His provision for it?

The most common objection to belief in the God of the *Bible* is that since He allows suffering, He cannot be good. But in light of the suffering which *God Himself endured* in order to make forgiveness, justification, and glorification possible, God is good *because* He was willing to suffer for us in order to atone for all the suffering we cause. Psychological studies confirm that soul suffering is more difficult to endure than physical suffering.[27] But in whatever form suffering comes, it speaks to us of the devastation caused by our lack of goodness: "[E]veryone has sinned, everyone falls short of the beauty of God's plan" (Romans 3:23 Phillips).

Human suffering is a key means by which God convinces us that there is something wrong which only He can make right. Our own destructive tendencies are often too unyielding to respond to anything else. And once a person becomes a Christian, bad things can still happen to them. This is true because we are still vulnerable to the forces of nature and choices of our fellow humans. But it is also true because Christians are still tempted and sometimes fall. In those cases, God corrects them in order to restore them (Hebrews 12:5-11). And whether suffering is the result of chastening or is no fault of their own, God will use it to accomplish good.

Many events recorded in the *Bible* illustrate this principle. Think of Job, Joseph, Elijah, David, Jeremiah, the Apostles, and Jesus Himself. Among other things, suffering can be used to alleviate the suffering of others, as in the case of Joseph, who told his brothers who had sent him into slavery: "Even though you planned evil against me, God planned good to come out of it. This was to keep many people alive, as he is doing now" (Genesis 50:20 GWT). Or suffering can be used to develop godly character, as in the case of Paul, who noted that God did not heal him of what the Apostle described as a "thorn in my flesh, a messenger from Satan to torment me" because it would "keep me from becoming proud" (II Corinthians 12:7 NLT).

And to non-Christians observing the lives of Christians, and even at times to Christians themselves, the suffering which God allows certain Christians to be subjected to seems pointless and excessive. Certainly it casts doubt on the assertion that God is loving and good. And don't we need all of our faculties to minister most effectively for our Lord? Think of the opportunities to advance His Kingdom by being able to share daily devotionals internationally, to promote the goodness of God on radio and television, to encourage people through in-person ministry and artistic creations, and even to bring practical help to disabled people around the world.

Yet all of these types of ministries are being successfully carried out by a Christian who suffered the physical, emotional, and spiritual anguish of becoming a quadriplegic in the prime of life. But by clinging to God, trusting that He would bring good out of bad, Joni Eareckson Tada became an effective minister of the Gospel, and an internationally known advocate for the needs of the physically disabled.[28] Yes, THERE'S ALWAYS MORE TO EVERY STORY.

Business as Usual?

―――――――――――＋✦✦✦✦✦＋――――――――――

By turning away from God, we humans have dug a pit from which we have been unable to extricate ourselves. Nevertheless, we continue to try to work our way out. We have turned to science and technology to address the problems we encounter in the physical world. Primitive techniques of acquiring water and food are superseded by increasingly sophisticated methods of rain making, desalinization, agriculture, and means of distribution. Goods made by hand in labor-intensive cottage industries give way to goods mass-produced as a result of the industrial revolution. Manpower, horsepower, and waterpower are replaced by steam power, fossil fuel power, electric power, solar power, and nuclear power.

And while many benefits can be traced to these changes, it seems there is always collateral damage as well. For example, every new source of power brings its own set of problems, from the negative effects of extracting fossil fuels to the challenge of disposing of nuclear waste. And our efforts to increase the availability of water and food, and to create new products designed to lighten our burdens, have also generated harmful chemicals and brought about other changes that have damaged our lives and environment.

As Lesslie Newbigin points out in his book, *Foolishness to the Greeks*, before the industrial revolution largely displaced them, cottage industries provided each worker with a direct connection to the finished product. Quality products brought in local customers and built worker prestige. But since the Industrial Revolution, worker prestige and the quality of products have too often taken a back seat to the bottom line. Since greater profits are obtainable through the economics of scale, international distribution, use of inferior materials, planned obsolescence, and advertising campaigns which appeal to human weaknesses, business administrators are frequently expected to leave their ethics at the door, and workers are relegated to the status of replaceable cogs in an endless cycle of production and consumption.[29]

As Canadian philosopher Marshall McLuhan famously summarized in his statement "the medium is the message," every new extension of human capabilities through technology or other means brings changes to society which are separate and distinct from what these new capabilities enable us to do.[30] Thus the industrial revolution, for example, increased the speed and scale of production, but led to the loss of worker prestige and an undue emphasis on the bottom line. Ever since we turned away from God, the technological advances we developed to work our way out of the pit we find ourselves in regularly produce consequences which extend far beyond material considerations to matters of the soul.

It seems that God never intended us to be problem-free in this life. Although we are dependent on our natural environment to sustain our lives, we are also subject to its destructive side. Over the centuries man has developed ways of reducing that destruction, but we find that our efforts are no match for the devastation that the universe is capable of unleashing. Earthquakes, volcanic eruptions, hurricanes, tornadoes, floods, and tsunamis threaten us from within; and meteors, asteroids, cosmic radiation, and the incineration of our planet as the sun expands into a red giant, threaten us from without.

However, we ourselves are responsible for digging the pit we find ourselves in. The very air we breathe—the breath of life—is never in short supply in our atmosphere, although at times events such as sandstorms and forest fires may render it difficult to access. But from the time we first gathered around campfires we have managed to find our own ways to pollute it. The Green Revolution is touted

15

as an essential effort to clean up and conserve earth's resources, but unfortunately it can also be a smokescreen for increasing somebody's bottom line and creating a new set of problems.

Yet not all human efforts to ease man's burdens disregard the potential collateral damage. The *Bible* in fact addresses this issue in the context of specific vocations. For example, tradespeople are accountable to use accurate measures as they conduct business. Thus, *Scripture* emphasizes the role that morals play in business decisions. And being truthful and respecting human dignity are two of the most important ones. As Francis Shaeffer put it, although it will not be until we are conformed to the image of Christ in the new heavens and earth that we will be completely raised from the pit, following God's commandments in the here and now will result in a "substantial healing" which significantly reduces negative consequences.[31]

But in our desire to play God, we are inclined to disregard God's rules and create our own. And sadly, these humanly devised rules are prominent in our day and age as we look to technology and the cycle of production and consumption to pull us out of the pit, rather than to God's provision of a "new heart" (Ezekiel 36:26 NIV). We find that the economy is typically the main issue of our societal concerns and political campaigns. Obviously, loving God, neighbor, and self, has economic implications. In fact, one of the Ten Commandments specifically addresses the issue of economic accountability.

But those who are determined to play by their own set of rules implicitly endorse an economic commandment of their own. And because it promotes the *driving force* behind an endless cycle of production and consumption based on fallen human nature, it is a commandment which encourages disregard for the collateral damage it causes. That driving force? . . . covetousness; and the "commandment" that sanctions it? . . . "Thou *shalt* covet."[32] The choice is ours. Yes, THERE'S ALWAYS MORE TO EVERY STORY.

Cattle Call

Whether mental health struggles are considered mental illnesses depends on the degree to which they interfere with normal life behaviors. Many of us experience such struggles without ever needing restorative help. "But some people experience feelings of anxiety or depression or suffer mood swings that are so severe and overwhelming that they interfere with personal relationships, job responsibilities, and daily functioning."[33]

One study lists anxiety disorders, major depressive disorders, and bipolar disorder as the three most common mental disorders in the US.[34] And to further complicate matters, those suffering from mental illness frequently manifest more than one type of disorder at the same time. The factors contributing to mental illness include genetic tendencies, sources of stress, and personal choices. And exactly if and how any of these is involved in a particular individual can be difficult to determine. But we must keep in mind that today there are medical and spiritual approaches which can be highly effective in treating these more common varieties of mental disorder.[35]

On the opposite end of the spectrum there are mental illnesses—or various expressions of delusional disorders—that are rare and can be extremely difficult or not yet possible to treat. Most of them are unfamiliar to the general public and characterized by unbelievably bizarre symptoms. Among them are Alice in Wonderland Syndrome, in which the sufferer's perception of reality becomes distorted so that objects appear larger or smaller than they really are, sounds louder or softer, movement faster or slower, etc.; Alien Hand Syndrome, in which one hand or arm is no longer under the body's control and attempts to harm the victim and others; and Paris Syndrome, which occurs temporarily each year among visitors to Paris, mainly Japanese, causing them to experience tremendous anxiety and severe delusions.[36]

Most of us have heard fanciful tales of people transforming into wolves or werewolves. But Clinical Lycanthropy is a very real delusional state in which victims believe they are wolves and behave accordingly, even living in isolated woodlands.[37] Less well-known is Boanthropy. In this very rare delusional state, individuals become convinced they are bovines—cows or oxen! Not only do victims moo like cows, walk around on all fours, join a herd, and chomp contentedly on cow feed, some may even insist that they be allowed to fulfill a cow's destiny in a butcher shop! And at present there is no standard method available for treating it. Clinicians must treat each case with open and perceptive minds.[38]

Among the most outlandish, yet insightful, methods of restorative therapy in the annals of mental illness involved a severely depressed man who believed that his life as a cow would never be fulfilled until his flesh was available in a butcher shop:

> [There] are few cows fatter than me in town. If the
> chef cooked "harissa" (goulash) of my meat, his
> pocket would turn into a silver treasure. Hurry, cut
> my throat, take me to the butchery.[39]

All efforts to change his outlook failed, and he began losing weight, finally refusing to eat altogether. It was then that Avicenna, the Islamic Hippocrates of the Golden Age of Islam (800-1258 A.D.), was called upon to help:[40]

[Avicenna said], "[G]o and tell him that tomorrow morning, the chief butcher will come to slaughter you knife in hand." On hearing the good news, the patient rejoiced and became excited. In the morning Avicenna went to the patient's house shouting, "Where is the cow?" The patient came out, laid down in the middle of the yard, saying "I am the cow, such and such come forward." Abu Ali [Avicenna] bound his hands and feet firmly, sharpened his knives and sat down. As a butcher would measure an animal, Avicenna inspected him and stroked his sides and back.

Afterwards, Avicenna said, this "cow is still undernourished; it is not wise to kill him today. Feed it for some time, never let it go hungry. When it is fat enough, I shall draw the blade, so its slaughter is not a waste." They untied his hands and feet and put food in front of him. Everything they gave to him of food and medicine he took and ate without resistance, so, as [a cow], he [would] gain weight. Eventually, the delusion of being a cow faded away.[41]

Boanthropy is no respecter of persons. Both small and great may suffer from it. According to the *Bible,* boanthropy not only has causes and effects, but also specific purposes. Again, the conditions contributing to any particular delusional state may be difficult to ascertain. But in at least one case, boanthropy did result from the failure of a prideful warrior-king to "acknowledge that the Most High is sovereign over all kingdoms on earth and gives them to anyone he wishes" (Daniel 4:32 NIV). Strolling one day on the roof of his palace, King Nebuchadnezzar boasted:

> Is not this the great Babylon I have built as the royal
> residence, by my mighty power and for the glory of
> my majesty? (Daniel 4:30 NIV).

Undoubtedly, many factors played into Nebuchadnezzar becoming the man he was. But in any case, a voice from heaven informed the mighty king who had destroyed Jerusalem and led Judah into captivity:

> You will be driven away from people and will live
> with the wild animals; you will eat grass like the ox
> (Daniel 4:25 NIV).

And that is exactly what happened! It took seven years, but Nebuchadnezzar learned his lesson. His sanity and kingdom were restored, and he at last acknowledged the One true God:

> Now I, Nebuchadnezzar, praise and exalt and
> glorify the King of heaven, because everything he
> does is right and all his ways are just. And those
> who walk in pride he is able to humble (Daniel
> 4:37 NIV).

And yes, THERE'S ALWAYS MORE TO EVERY STORY.

Change of Heart

The heart is located in the approximate center of the chest, and since the time of Aristotle in ancient Greece it was considered the most important organ in the body. Not only was it believed to be the strongest muscle in the body, but also the location of the mind, and the control center for all bodily functions. By 1700 the anatomy of the heart and its role in pumping oxygenated blood throughout the body and removing cellular waste was well understood.[42] Further study of the other internal organs, however, has revealed that all organs interact, and no part—even the heart—is accountable for every essential function.

As the Apostle Paul put it centuries before:

> If the whole body were an eye, where would the sense of hearing be? If the whole body were an ear, where would the sense of smell be? . . . But God has put the body together . . . so that there should be no division in the body, but that its parts should have equal concern for each other. If one part suffers, every part suffers with it; if one part is honored, every part rejoices with it. (I Corinthians 12:17, 24-26 NIV)

Just so, while the heart provides vital transportation to and from the brain, by means of nerve cell connections the brain stimulates the heart to keep on beating. Without the brain, the heart would eventually cease to beat, and without the heart, the brain would begin to become irreparably damaged within as little as three minutes! The effectiveness of CPR and defibrillation depends on how quickly they are applied.[43]

Furthermore, there's reportedly evidence of another key connection between heart and brain. It seems that the heart is more than just a pump after all! In fact, the terms "heart brain," "little brain," and "intrinsic cardiac nervous system" refer to a dense cluster of neurons (nerve cells) located in one portion of the heart. These neurons are connected to the brain and apparently send more messages to the brain than the brain sends to the heart. While the brain is the organ of rational thought, processing and storing sensory input, "the heart is considered the source of emotions, desire, and wisdom . . . [and] is probably a key moderator of pain."[44] If so, while the "head brain" does the thinking, the "heart brain" controls other vital aspects of a person's psyche.

Whether or not all of these conclusions pan out, a healthy brain and a healthy heart are unquestionably essential to our overall well-being. One of the possible contributors to an *unhealthy* brain and an *unhealthy* heart are psychosomatic disorders. Such disorders result when mental stresses negatively affect bodily functions. Studies of the relationship between the brain-heart connection and sudden death have shown that both intense fear and intense excitement can cause the heart to stop beating. These studies suggest the mechanism by which "voodoo curses" can cause death in a superstitious society by producing extreme fear.[45]

As such a crucial organ, the heart *must* keep beating. But no heart beats forever. On December 3, 1967, the first successful human heart transplant was performed in Cape Town, South Africa, by Doctor Christiaan Barnard and an extensive surgical team. The patient lived for only 18 hours, but since then, techniques have greatly improved. As of 2021, the longest that anyone has lived after a heart transplant is 35 years. And a number have had a second and even a third heart transplant.[46]

But what about artificial hearts? After besting actor Ricardo Montalban in a "dance-off" on the Arthur Murray Dance Party program, popular vaudeville and television ventriloquist Paul Winchell met Dr. Henry Heimlich (inventor of the Heimlich maneuver) at a cast party. They became good friends, and Heimlich invited Winchell to observe some of his open-heart surgeries. Winchell, whose many talents included coming up with inventions for which he obtained over 30 patents during his lifetime, decided then and there to try his hand at making an artificial heart that could be used to keep blood flowing during open heart surgeries. Consulting with Heimlich along the way, he designed and built a prototype of an artificial heart and obtained the first patent on such a devise in 1963.[47]

Others have improved upon Winchell's design over the years, and the artificial heart is now primarily used to keep blood flowing until a suitable human heart becomes available to transplant. A relatively small number of patients have not been able to receive a heart transplant due to age or preexisting conditions, but by 2020 some have survived up to ten years with an artificial heart.[48]

However, contrary to popular belief, heart replacement surgery actually dates back to the earliest years of human history and has an unmatched record of success! As the first organ to develop in the human embryo, it seems appropriate that in the *Bible* the word "heart" is most often used figuratively to mean "the driving force behind our character, decisions, words and deeds"[49]:

> Above all else, guard your heart, for everything you do flows from it" (Proverbs 4:23 NIV). "A good man brings good things out of the good stored up in his heart, and an evil man brings evil things out of the evil stored up in his heart" (Luke 6:45 NIV).

Yet the LORD says, "The heart is deceitful above all things and beyond cure" (Jeremiah 17:9 BSB). But as the Great Physician, God offers to surgically remove our "heart of stone" and give us a "heart of flesh" (Ezekiel 36:26 NIV). The survival rate from this once-in-a-lifetime procedure is 100%, and the longevity of this new heart is eternal! Yes, THERE'S ALWAYS MORE TO EVERY STORY.

Contending for the Faith

--- ✦✦✦✦✦ ---

The Battle For the Bible is both the title of a widely read Christian book and a concise appraisal of the situation which has developed in the realm of Biblical theology.[50] The title suggests the intensity of the conflict between those who hold to the doctrine of Biblical inerrancy—that "All *Scripture* is given by inspiration of God" (II Timothy 3:16 KJV)—and those who would limit or qualify the extent to which the writings of *Scripture* can be trusted as the very Word of God. And the battle is only the latest outbreak in an age-old conflict.

Its roots can be traced to the very first point of contention recorded in *Genesis*: "Indeed, has God said, 'You shall not eat from any tree of the garden?" (Genesis 3:1 NASB). Satan began by sowing the seeds of doubt in Eve's mind, then quickly followed up with an outright contradiction of what she readily acknowledged to be God's Word. First raising doubts about what parts of *Scripture* are unquestionably the words of God, then launching a brazen frontal attack on the integrity of what remains, Satan's strategy has stayed remarkably consistent down through the centuries.

Yet in every age, God has raised up faithful men and women to "contend earnestly for the faith which was once for all delivered to the saints" (Jude 1:3 NKJV). At times, the faithful were few in number—the eight souls preserved in the ark, the seven thousand who along with Elijah had not bowed their knees to Baal, the remnant whom God always preserved in times of national declension. But God saw to it that their faith remained intact in the face of all efforts on the part of the enemy to destroy it. Doubts were allayed, heresies put down, the *Scriptures* shared, the needy ministered to, justice done, persecution endured, and God glorified!

From the time of Israel's birth as a nation, her people had been repeatedly warned of the dangers posed by the false religious systems of other cultures. And often throughout the nation's history she had failed to heed those warnings and had suffered dreadfully. Seventy years into their captivity in Babylon, Jews were allowed to return to Palestine to rebuild Jerusalem and the temple. Since then, the nation had made a slow and rocky recovery. And although she was still functioning at the discretion of a succession of foreign powers, the foreign rule had been somewhat benevolent, and she had been allowed a good measure of self-determination. However, when Greece took over Palestine, it sought to compel Jews to adopt Greek culture–to Hellenize them.

It was at this critical juncture that a company of the faithful who contended earnestly for the faith–the Chasidim–emerged to stand in the gap, defending the faith, zealously affirming the truth of *Scripture*. And their zeal did not falter when a change in foreign rule placed Israel in the tyrannical grip of a dictator who set out to displace Judaism and destroy the *Scriptures*. Subsequent persecution only served to draw the Chasidim closer together and strengthen their resolve to stand firm for the Word of God. Many suffered death for their uncompromising stand, yet in the end, their resistance to those forces which would destroy God's Word, and their unflagging support of Israeli freedom fighters, helped bring independence once more to the nation. Later, when a new party of Israeli political leaders sought to turn the nation in an increasingly secular direction, the Chasidim once more stood firm for God's Word, this time suffering persecution at the hands of their own countrymen.[51]

Yes, the battle for the *Bible* is really a war of long standing. And the Chasidim are among its greatest heroes, though readers of the *New Testament* might never suspect it. For you see, many of the Chasidim–the "saints"–who had contended so valiantly for the faith amidst the impact of Greek culture and the violence of arch enemy Antiochus Epiphanes, had, over a succession of generations, exchanged truth for political power.[52] They had become those for whom the Lord Jesus reserved his most scathing criticism and who subsequently had Him crucified, those Chasidim—better known as Pharisees—who rejected Him! Yes, THERE'S ALWAYS MORE TO EVERY STORY.

Does the Bible Get It Wrong?

✦✦✦✦✦✦

The *Bible* is not a book of science. In fact, many critics argue that lack of scientific accuracy in biblical accounts clearly refutes claims of Divine origin. After all, if God inspired the *Bible's* human authors with both its propositions and the very words used to express them, why wouldn't references to the workings of the Creation be scientifically accurate? While we can excuse these human authors for their ignorance of the "facts" of modern science, wouldn't the wordings which God supplied reflect His alleged omniscience?

But if the *Bible* is not a book of science–which obviously it is not–is scientific accuracy essential to its intended purpose? Besides–and it is crucial that we bear this in mind–what is accepted as scientifically correct today is likely to be *modified or replaced* tomorrow. And if God did supply *final explanations* for the physical phenomena mentioned in *Scripture*, perhaps even the greatest scientists of our times, let alone any other *Bible* readers, would be hard-pressed to comprehend them. In that case, the writings inspired by an omnipotent God who is expected to provide an accurate picture of the way Creation works, *would not serve the purpose for which He inspired them*!

Scripture is, after all, a communication from God telling us about Himself, His love for Creation–His handiwork–our special role as His image bearers, our accountability for the choices we make, and the opportunity we have to be made right with Him forever. And He addresses us holistically, speaking to our entire being: spirit, mind, will, emotions, body. Thus it was essential that these truths be presented in terms to which all those who hear or read the *Bible* can relate. Those who were first to hear or read portions of *Scripture* lived in cultures different in many ways from our own, yet similar enough that the message which the *Bible* conveys speaks to all people in all times and situations. Thus its forty authors used a variety of literary genres–primarily narrative, poetry, wisdom, and prophecy–to express that message.

Statements in narrative are predominantly "literal," simply "telling what's happening." The other three genres contain an abundance of "figurative" language, using metaphors and other literary devices to express ideas. Those readers familiar with astronomy would not take a reference to the rising or setting sun as an assertion that the sun revolves around the Earth! If they did, the purpose of the statement might be completely missed and the validity of *Scripture* wrongly denied. And although *Scripture* encourages scientific effort–in fact, a biblical worldview arguably initiated the age of modern science[53]–it is primarily concerned with whether that effort is *properly bounded and applied* as we exercise freedom of choice.

Certainly, the *Bible* tells of many incidents which defy scientific explanation. At particular times, especially during the ministry of Jesus, miracles were employed by God to authenticate the Divine authority behind words and deeds. At most times, however, God works *behind the scenes* as He interacts with Creation. He is nevertheless sovereign, sometimes intervening on our behalf, including stepping in to restrain our ill-advised choices, and other times allowing us to experience fully the consequences, good or bad, of our situations.

God has made us rational beings possessing the ability to make sensory observations and detect regular patterns within the physical aspect of reality, to trace the paths–as A.W. Tozer points out–along which God consistently directs His power.[54] These are the paths commonly referred to as the "laws of nature." Our knowledge of these paths enables us to predict physical outcomes and thus helps us fulfill the roles God assigned us in the beginning: to act as Earth's stewards and to develop culture (Genesis 1:28).

And it would be a grave error to conclude that science is any less a *supernatural revelation from God* than any of His other revelations, since He provides the sensory apparatus by which we observe, the reasoning ability by which we draw conclusions, and–of course– maintains the patterns which scientists discover. All of these forms of revelation are primarily designed to further acquaint us with the holiness and character of God, and our accountability as His image bearers.

But couldn't He have provided insights, or at least hints, which would have enhanced human flourishing *long before* the age of science? Take the field of health, for instance. Modern medical research has provided knowledge which is being applied in our times to deal with health crises such as COVID-19. Had the people in *Bible* times known about the germ theory of disease, recognized symptoms of disease, understood how contagious diseases are spread, regularly practiced hand washing, appreciated the value of quarantining, realized the importance of potable water, and implemented proper methods of sewage disposal, their health could have been significantly improved. *And indeed it was*, because among *Bible*-believing people in pre-scientific times, *all of these health practices were documented in Scripture, long before modern science established their scientific grounds.* Yes, THERE'S ALWAYS MORE TO EVERY STORY.

Down to the Sea in Ships

—— ✦✦✦✦✦ ——

The Age of the Ocean Liner extended over more than a century, from the mid-1800s to the mid-1900s. In the early 1800s, the Industrial Revolution greatly increased the need for regular and dependable transportation between continents, both for securing raw materials and distributing finished products, and to convey passengers including government and business personnel. In 1818, a British shipping company began regularly scheduled passenger service between England and the United States via sailing ship. But by the middle of the century the steam engine had replaced the sail as the primary means of ship propulsion:[55]

> As steamships were less dependent on wind patterns, new trade routes opened up. The steamship has been described as a 'major driver of the first wave of trade globalization (1870–1913)' and contributor to 'an increase in international trade that was unprecedented in human history.'[56]

One of the greatest civil engineers of the time, England's Isambard Kingdom Brunel, determined that the fuel required to move a ship did not increase as rapidly as the ship's size did. Thus, the larger the ship, the more profitable it would be.[57] The only problem was that wooden ships could not safely exceed three hundred feet in length. But the problem was solved as wood was replaced by iron, and eventually by steel, in ship construction.[58]

However, the amount of fuel required to power such ships limited the distance they could travel between fuel stops. This difficulty was overcome by the invention of the steam turbine, which not only burned less fuel but was also much easier to maintain.[59] The first large commercial vessel to use the steam turbine was the British ocean liner RMS Victorian, launched in 1904. At a length of 520 feet, it performed admirably, plying the Atlantic between Britain and the US, serving as an armed warship during WWI, and afterwards resuming service in a civilian capacity.[60] Three years later the British Cunard Line's RMS Mauretania was launched. She was the world's largest ship for the next five years, with a length of 790 feet. And at 28 mph, she was the fastest, a record she held for over twenty years.[61]

In 1911 and 1912 the first two members of a new class of ships were launched for service on the British White Star Line. Rather than compete with the Mauretania in speed, White Star chose to emphasize luxury. The second of these Olympic Class liners broke the record for largest passenger ship, at a length of 883 feet and a volume of 4,632,800 cubic feet. But the record was short-lived because the RMS Titanic sank on her maiden voyage. Two hours and forty minutes after colliding with an iceberg, the ship went down. Over 1500 of the 2200-plus on board perished.[62]

The ship that one White Star employee allegedly said even God couldn't sink, was actually sunk due to the fallibility of its designers and the carelessness of its operators. The number of lifeboats available was woefully inadequate, and those that were launched were not always full.[63] Furthermore, although the loss of life could have been dramatically reduced if the nearby SS California had responded to the Titanic's distress signals, it failed to do so.[64]

But there is another side to this story. During those two hours and forty minutes, many heroic deeds were performed, most by people who would lose their lives in the process. "Women and children first" was the imperative as the lifeboats were loaded, and the men aboard the Titanic selflessly strove to see them safely away.[65] The most widely remembered act of sacrificial service was that of the string ensemble of eight musicians who played throughout the chaos on board. As the Titanic slipped beneath the water, many survivors reported that the musicians were playing the hymn "Nearer My God to Thee." None of these musicians survived.[66] Of ensemble leader Wallace Hartley, a musician friend later said:

> I don't suppose he waited to be sent for, but after finding how dangerous the situation was he probably called his men together and began playing. I know that he often said that music was a bigger weapon for stopping disorder than anything on earth. He knew the value of the weapon he had, and I think he proved his point.[67]

Hartley and the other ensemble members were churchgoing men who, in the words of a New York City Pastor, "died a death worth dying, to teach us how to live a life worth living."[68]

But there was also a lesser-known act of sacrificial love on that day that should be mentioned. Pastor John Harper was traveling with his daughter to the US to preach at the Moody Memorial Church in Chicago and accept an invitation to become its new pastor. When the collision occurred, he made sure his daughter was safely aboard a lifeboat, then spent the rest of the time before the ship sank going person to person sharing the Gospel. And he continued to do so even as he swam among others in the icy water. A man clinging to a board was encouraged by Harper to believe in Jesus, but refused to do so as he drifted off. Shortly afterwards, the same man passed by again and was similarly entreated, just before Harper slipped beneath the waves.[69]

Four years later in a meeting of Titanic survivors, a gentleman identified himself as the man clinging to the board whom Harper had twice pled with to "Believe in the Lord Jesus Christ." He recounted that he was rescued by a lifeboat which had turned back to look for survivors, and he identified himself as "the last convert of John Harper."[70] Yes, THERE'S ALWAYS MORE TO EVERY STORY.

Duality Disorder

+ + ✦ ✦ ✦ + +

The scope of Jesus' healing ministry takes in both body and spirit. And neither aspect of man's nature is to be considered nonessential. Both spirit and body will always be interacting aspects of human beings in the Kingdom of God, including Jesus–God incarnate. When the good work which God has begun in us is completed on the day of the Lord Jesus Christ, we will be fully conformed to the image of His Son, not only in spirit but in body as well: "[Jesus] will transform our lowly bodies so that they will be like his glorious body (Philippians 3:21 NIV).

And Jesus' earthly ministry primarily involved teaching and healing. Those who were healed by Him were beneficiaries of the means by which Jesus publicly established His divine authority–that He was indeed the Messiah. And His healings were not limited to the body alone, but indicated Jesus' desire to "restore the whole person to God."[71] Thus, His healings ran the gamut, from meeting emotional needs to raising the dead to saving souls. In the twenty-two healings recorded in the synoptic gospels (Matthew, Mark, and Luke), Jesus' more often healed the poor. Alvin Lloyd Maragh asserts:

> In the Bible, the poor are not merely those who suffer from material poverty, they are also the oppressed, the exploited, the despised, and the marginalized. The term poor is often used synonymously with

35

> the word oppressed. The Bible identifies injustice
> and oppression as the main causes of poverty and
> indicates its systemic nature. . . . Besides Jesus'
> ministry to the marginalized, His healing ministry
> also addressed theological issues of sin and salvation,
> the issue of Sabbath keeping, and the importance of
> the role of faith.[72]

Conditions which call for healing have been present ever since humans first rebelled against God. All of us need the spiritual healing of our relationship with God. Often as a result of a person's sin, natural consequences cause them to need other types of healing as well. For example, sexual sin may result in STDs or threaten to destroy a family. However, at other times a person may suffer from conditions which they have incurred through no fault of their own.

And since we are both spirit and body, physical disorders have implications for spiritual health, and spiritual disorders have implications for physical health. Jesus healed miraculously, but those healings also had a ripple effect which resulted in other healings. For instance, the lepers whose disease was cured were also no longer subject to the social and emotional isolation from which they had also suffered.

And God has enabled us to discover "natural laws" of cause-and-effect which can lead to prevention and healing of some of the conditions which Jesus healed miraculously. Thus, knowledge of these "natural" laws–"the paths along which God consistently directs His power"[73]–allows us to act as His coworkers in the business of physical healing.

And because we have learned much since *Bible* times about the role of body chemistry and other factors in emotional pain and mental disorders, why should Christians be hesitant to use therapy and medication to help alleviate them? Why should we hesitate to use them any more than we would hesitate to treat certain contagious diseases with antiseptic techniques and antibiotics? Christians who tend to blame suffering from physical and psychological conditions on an individual's sin or lack of faith should consider Jesus' miracles of healing more carefully.

He made it clear that whether or not suffering is the result of a sufferer's sin or lack of faith, it *always* contributes to the fulfillment of God's higher purposes.[74] Although the very *existence* of suffering among humans is due to the sin of Adam, suffering is the very *means* by which suffering will ultimately be eliminated!

> When Adam sinned, sin entered the world. Adam's sin brought death, so death spread to everyone, for everyone sinned. (Romans 5:12 NLT). But God showed his great love for us by sending Christ to die for us while we were still sinners (Romans 5:8 NLT).

Many *Bible* characters suffered from deep feelings of loss, sadness, and loneliness, including Job, Moses, Elijah, David, and even Jesus. Jesus expressed emotions because He was fully man as well as fully God, and emotions are an aspect of God's image in human beings. He cried at the death of Lazarus, mourned over the unbelief of the people of Jerusalem, was angered by those who made His Father's house a den of thieves, pled with His Father in the Garden of Gethsemane, and cried out in agony on the cross because his Father had forsaken Him. Yet each of these instances played a vital role in a plan culminating in inexpressible joy. Jesus told his disciples:

> When you obey my commandments, you remain in my love, just as I obey my Father's commandments and remain in his love. I have told you these things so that you will be filled with my joy. Yes, your joy will overflow! (John 15:10 and 11 NLT)

Because of the joy awaiting him, he endured the cross (Hebrews 12:2 NLT).

God doesn't allow His followers to be free of physical and emotional pain. The apostle Paul had a thorn in the flesh which wasn't removed. God explained that "because of the extraordinary character of the revelations" He had given Paul, he allowed him to suffer a "thorn in the flesh, . . . a messenger of Satan to trouble [him]—so that [he] would not become arrogant." Paul elaborates: "I asked the Lord three times about this, that it would depart from me. But he said to me, "My grace is enough for you, for my power is made perfect in weakness." (II Corinthians 12:7-9 NET).

Well-known English pastor Charles Haddon Spurgeon, the "Prince of Preachers," had bouts of deep depression, especially in his later years. But these were not necessarily brought on by sin or lack of faith, but simply came unbidden, taking a terrible toll. Nevertheless, Spurgeon accomplished great things for God.[75]

All of us may experience deep feelings of loss, sadness, loneliness, and other painful emotions, sometimes due to sin or lack of faith, but certainly not always so. On the other hand, there is also clinical or major depression which has a variety of causes and typically must be addressed in our day both medically–through therapy and medication–and spiritually–through prayer, *Bible* study, and spiritual counsel. Yet, Christians can suffer from mental illnesses, including major depression, without losing their usefulness to God.

Consider the life of Charlotte Elliot. Born in England in 1789, she was full of zest for life. In her youth she was a talented painter and writer of humorous verse. But in her early thirties she was afflicted with a physical disorder which left her bedridden and suffering from depression and personal guilt. She was convinced she needed to "clean up her act" in order to become a Christian. However, a visiting pastor from Switzerland assured her that each person who comes to God is welcome just as they are; Jesus had already taken care of the rest.

Years later, now a Christian, Charlotte suffered from perhaps her worst bout of depression, even questioning her own salvation. Then she recalled the Swiss pastor's words and began to write the text of the best-known of her nearly 150 hymns: "Just As I Am."[76] This hymn was playing when young Billy Graham committed his life to Christ:

> Just as I am, without one plea
> But that Thy blood was shed for me
> And that Thou bid'st me come to Thee
> O Lamb of God, I come! I come![77]

Graham subsequently used it in most of his Crusades as attendees were invited forward to commit their lives to the Lord. Graham said that "Just As I Am" "presented the strongest possible Biblical basis for the call of Christ." And *Hymnody* historian Kenneth Osbeck wrote that "Just As I Am" had "touched more hearts and influenced more people for Christ than any other song ever written."[78] Yes, THERE'S ALWAYS MORE TO EVERY STORY.

Education 101

In today's culturally chaotic times, disinformation, misinformation, half-truths, fabrications, false news, and bald-faced lies seem to be the rule rather than the exception. But in human experience they date back to the Garden of Eden. A "teacher" appears in the Garden in the guise of a snake, and employs deception to raise doubts about the truthfulness of God's Word. Sadly, Satan's impersonation of a concerned and scholarly rational being is so convincing that it plants seeds of doubt in Eve's mind. And when Eve gives in to Satan's deception, Adam chooses *her* over God. From then on education becomes tainted by sin.

Over the millennia, the educational system has expanded, and any part of this system can be corrupted by sin. To what extent is primarily determined by the willingness of those shaping that system to incorporate biblical principles. Christian teachers must not only know the Word of God intellectually but apply it actively. And Christian educators, beginning with parents and including all persons involved in the educational system, have the opportunity and responsibility to teach their students what it means to think and act Christianly, and to introduce them to the power to do so.

Educational institutions have unprecedented opportunities to influence the way young people think and act. Consider the oldest college in the United States, Harvard, founded in 1636, even *before* there was a United States. Harvard's original mission statement was:

> Let every student be plainly instructed and earnestly
> pressed to consider well the end of his life and studies
> is to know God and Jesus Christ, which is eternal
> life, and therefore to lay Christ in the bottom, as
> the only foundation of all sound knowledge and
> learning.[79]

Ten of Harvard's first twelve presidents were ministers of the Gospel, and whether its students were training to become pastors or not, the vast majority sought to make Christ their foundation of "knowledge and learning."[80] Throughout its first fifty years the Massachusetts Bay Colony in which Harvard was located was predominantly Puritan and Congregationalist–orthodox Christian. Harvard's original motto clearly reflected that orthodoxy: "Truth for Christ and the Church."[81]

But times were changing. Unitarianism, which rejected the triune nature of God and the divinity of Christ, was becoming the school's dominant religious position. As part of this change, increasing emphasis was placed on the power of reason and the role of free will in directing human progress.

> In 1807 "The liberal Samuel Webber was appointed
> to the presidency of Harvard, which signaled
> the changing of the tide from the dominance of
> traditional ideas at Harvard to the dominance of
> liberal . . . Unitarian ideas."[82]

The last clergyman to be president of Harvard completed his term in 1868 and was succeeded by Harvard's most innovative and longest serving president, Charles Eliot. During his forty-year stint, Eliot:

> eliminated the favored position of Christianity
> from the curriculum while opening it to student

41

self-direction. . . . [H]e was motivated . . . by
transcendentalist Unitarian convictions . . . focused
on the dignity and worth of human nature, the
right and ability of each person to perceive truth
and the indwelling God in each person.[83] [Or if
one preferred, without the necessity of God at all.]

And as you know, this secular philosophy now dominates our
public educational system from preschool on.

Under Eliot's leadership, emphasis on theology and classical
learning was replaced by emphasis on the broader offerings of a
university education in which each student was encouraged to
explore their own gifts and interests. It was felt that they could then
focus on a subject area that would enable them to make the greatest
contribution to the progress of the human race. Eliot was convinced
there was a vital connection between such focused education and
the social, economic, political, and moral strength of the Nation.
During his tenure, Harvard became one of the most prestigious
universities in the world, and by far the most richly endowed. But
tellingly, among its various colleges, the Harvard Divinity School
was *poorly* endowed.[84]

On the positive side, Harvard is currently internationally known
for encouraging students to direct their own learning based on
their own gifts and interests, and for providing a wide variety of
curriculum choices with excellent research programs and a who's-
who of esteemed instructors.[85] But, as a secular university in
today's culture, Harvard, in concert with modern secular ideals,
welcomes a variety of worldviews and lifestyles as valid and capable
of contributing to social progress. Thus in 2019, for the very first
time, a higher percentage of freshmen identified as non-religious
than identified as Christians. One student commented:

Harvard students have not thoughtlessly become
indifferent toward religion. Rather, many have

reflected on its importance and concluded that it is not a prerequisite to the good and meaningful lives they are leading. . . . [Could anyone] suppose that the 37 percent of Harvard freshmen who do not believe in any higher entity are any less moral because of their beliefs? Any less apt to lead?[86]

Those who seek to discover the regular physical patterns of the universe and use that knowledge in beneficial ways are certainly *not* limited to orthodox Christians. All such persons thereby possess a certain *aptness to lead*. But the "degree" of *morality* exhibited by one group is not comparable to that of any other *unless there is an agreed upon standard of measure*. Otherwise, morality is merely whatever anyone chooses it to be. Consequently, with no agreed upon standard, anything is possible.

President Eliot believed that the graduates of a properly conceived university would inevitably advance human progress. Unquestionably, the German universities after which he had modeled Harvard produced highly educated, scientifically advanced, and outstandingly productive graduates,[87] . . . *but the Holocaust happened anyway!* Yes, THERE'S ALWAYS MORE TO EVERY STORY.

Flog or Golf?

--- ✦✦✦✦✦ ---

Many are called to play golf, but few are chosen to master it! Although games using a "golf" (a stick or club) and a "bag" or ball date back even further, the game of golf which we are familiar with today, incorporating 18 holes, originated in Scotland. The Old Links in Musselburgh, Scotland, on the coast near Edinburgh, is touted as the oldest course. But at first, playing golf was controversial. Governmental laws concerning the game of golf forbid its practice within towns because of the damage it caused, and at one time it was outlawed completely because it interfered with the archery practice needed for military readiness. Eventually, however, kings, queens and nobles joined in the competition.[88]

The Duke of Albany, later to become King James VII of Scotland, is credited with playing in the first international golf contest, in 1681. He and a partner played two English nobles for a substantial wager and the right to claim which was the game's country of origin. The winners? Well, the Duke's partner received enough money on the occasion to build a mansion on what is now known as Golfer's Land in Edinburgh![89]

Over the years, golf equipment has changed, most importantly the ball. Probably what was at first a wooden ball was replaced by a ball with a leather cover filled with hair, and, later, feathers; the "feathery" was replaced by a ball favored from 1848 until 1900 made of hardened tree sap (gutta percha); the "gutty" was replaced by a ball with a gutta percha cover enclosing a solid core wound in rubber strings; and this ball dominated golf until 1967 when the Spalding Golf Company substituted a synthetic cover for gutta percha. Variations in this design have proliferated greatly since then.[90]

And during this same period of development, it was gradually discovered that indentations which enhanced spin and control could be inscribed on a solid golf ball cover. The evolution of these indentations eventually resulted in the dimple patterns of modern golf balls.[91] Famed golfer Bobby Jones, winner of thirteen of the twenty-one major tournaments he played in during an unparalleled seven-year run, considered changes in the golf ball a key factor in the game's improvement.[92]

The oldest continuing golf tournament in history is The British Open, or simply, The Open. It is "open" in the sense that both qualifying professionals *and* amateurs can participate. First played in 1860, today it is one of the four preeminent golf tournaments known as the Majors. Bobby Jones won it three times over those storied seven years—as an amateur! And some of the best-known golfers in the world have their names inscribed on the Claret Jug commemorating its champions. But not all of those champions are flamboyant and constantly in the limelight, nor is their perception of championship golf necessarily the same as that of those golfers who primarily seek fame, fortune, and the "good" life.[93]

Of course, all of the contestants in golf tournaments are trying to win, but their back stories can differ widely. Consider Harris's story. Growing up he enjoyed a number of sports, from baseball to soccer. Around age ten he took up golf but thought of it as a hobby compared to his other sports activities.[94] However, he eventually changed his mind and began to focus on golf. Harris led his high school golf team to a state championship and had a successful collegiate golf career. Afterwards he turned pro and played on several developmental tours, eventually earning his ticket to the big one—the PGA Tour.

In his fourth year on the Tour, Harris became the first professional golfer since rankings have been kept to win the Masters

Tournament when ranked *outside* the top 50, besting Tiger Woods and two others by 2 strokes. Then, eight years later he won the British Open, becoming only the sixth golfer to win majors at both the Augusta National and St. Andrews courses.[95] His final round in that Open was a marvel of putting perfection and is considered one of the finest rounds ever played in that event.[96] In between his two majors, Harris became the first golfer to fire a 60 two-times on the PGA Tour, and won the Northwest Mutual World Challenge in a playoff, again beating Tiger Woods.[97]

So, what does a winning pro do with his substantial earnings? Many create charitable foundations and contribute generously to additional causes. Some, like Harris, follow this model because of the deep convictions that motivate their lives, rather than merely to come across as good guys.[98] And in 2020 Harris was chosen to receive the Payne Stewart Award "regarded as the most prestigious on the PGA Tour. . . . It goes to the player who best exemplifies Stewart's values of character, charity and sportsmanship."[99] After his Master's win, Harris–Zach Harris Johnson–publicly "mentioned his Christian faith and thanked God, saying: 'This being Easter, I cannot help but believe my Lord and Savior, Jesus Christ, was walking with me. I owe this to Him.'"[100] And other pro golfers, including Stewart Cink, Davis Love III, Bernhard Langer, Bubba Watson, Webb Simpson, Aaron Baddeley, and more, would say "Amen" to his words.[101] Yes, THERE'S ALWAYS MORE TO EVERY STORY.

Frequency

God has chosen to communicate with us in various ways including creation, conscience, prophets, angelic visits, dreams, and in person in Jesus. God spoke to Abraham in the form of a man and through angels and visions. He spoke to Moses through a burning bush, and to all of the freed Israeli slaves through the fire and thunder on Mt. Sinai. The Ten Commandments were inscribed on stone tablets by the finger of God. God also spoke through the mouth of a donkey when Balaam was traveling to the king of Moab to curse the Israelites on the king's behalf. And He spoke to Joshua as "the commander of the LORD's army," encouraging Joshua as he prepared to lead his fellow Israelites in the conquest of the Promised Land (Joshua 5:14 NLT).

God also spoke to Elijah in a "still small voice" when Elijah was fleeing from Ahab, the King of Israel (I Kings 19:12 NKJV). During the bondage of Judah in Babylon, God wrote with the "fingers of a disembodied human hand" on the wall of the King's banquet hall, warning of the nation's immanent overthrow (Daniel 7:5 and 6 The Message). Angelic appearances in person or in dreams also occur throughout the *New Testament*. And as Jesus approached Jerusalem on Palm Sunday, and His disciples loudly praised God for the miracles He had done through Jesus, some Pharisees asked Jesus to silence them. But Jesus told them, "[I]f they keep quiet, the stones will cry out" (Luke 19:40 NIV).

Yes, God has many ways of communicating with us, and we

are accountable to listen and respond appropriately. Claims to the contrary are mere rationalizations, fabricated in order to justify Satan's lie:

> [Y]ou will be like God. (Genesis 3:5 NIV).

> [Satan] . . . does not stand in the truth, because there is no truth in him. When he lies, he speaks out of his own character, for he is a liar and the father of lies. (John 8:44 ESV)

But although we are inherently bent on usurping our Creator's place, God continues to seek a hearing with us, substituting *truth* for lies. The liberty which many of us seek-after today is in fact *license* to determine our own values. While, as free moral agents, God allows us to make genuine choices, He at the same time offers us the truth which will liberate us from a slavery that, if left unchecked, will destroy us!

The *Bible* says that those who come to God "must believe that he exists and he rewards those who diligently search for him" (Hebrews 11:6 ISV). Furthermore, Jesus states that those who seek will find (Matthew 7:7). And Romans 1:18-23 makes it clear that those who claim they reject Christianity because of lack of evidence are actually *suppressing* that evidence:

> The wrath of God is being revealed from heaven against all the godlessness and wickedness of people, who suppress the truth by their wickedness, since what may be known about God is plain to them, because God has made it plain to them. For since the creation of the world God's invisible qualities– his eternal power and divine nature–have been clearly seen, being understood from what has been

made, so that people are without excuse. (Romans
1:18-20 NIV)

And as one ponders the ways in which God has communicated
with specific people, it is readily apparent that that communication is
precisely suited to each individual. Even when that communication
leads to saving faith, there are individual differences. For some,
conviction, confession, and conversion occur during a brief period
of personal crisis. For others, faith develops over a long period of
time. In every case the means are suited to the final goal—salvation
by grace through faith in Jesus.

Italian scientist Guglielmo Marconi is credited with the invention
of wireless communication over great distances using invisible
electromagnetic waves. We know this form of communication as
radio:[102]

> [A] member of the Anglican Church, . . . Marconi . . .
> pondered about how the human mind could bridge
> any distance, even reaching God in prayer. He was
> constantly writing about his amazement at God's
> creation, and how it was intertwined with science.
> You might say, Marconi was the first to envision
> religious broadcasting.[103]

Christian radio and television are among the means which
God uses today to communicate the Gospel to the world. Here
in the United States Moody Broadcasting, the ACN (American
Christian Network) stations, and TBN (The Trinity Broadcasting
Network) are prominent. HCJB (Heralding Christ Jesus' Blessings),
"The Voice of the Andes," was the first foreign-based Christian
radio station. FEBC (Far East Broadcasting Company) and TWR
(Trans World Radio) are other well-known Christian radio services
broadcasting abroad. And television and internet streaming have
further expanded the reach of the Gospel.

While technological advances make the Word of God available to a wider audience, even today some people claim that God speaks to them directly, revealing knowledge which enables them to immediately minister to the needs of others. Consider the Reverend Peter Popoff. Popoff attracted large numbers of people to his healing services, which were videoed for later broadcast. During these services he would identify people in need of healing from any of a variety of ills: physical, emotional, and spiritual. His detailed knowledge of where such people were located in his audience, their names, and their specific circumstances brought gasps and tears.[104]

Yet in these types of situations all may not be as it seems. Jesus said, "For false messiahs and false prophets will rise up and perform signs and wonders so as to deceive, if possible, even God's chosen ones" (Mark 13:22 NLT). It turned out that a group of skeptical researchers managed to record some of the conversations between Popoff and "God." Those conversations utilized a frequency of 39.17 MHz, in a bandwidth reserved for public emergency services including police, fire, and ambulance—certainly an appropriate bandwidth for emergency services from God!

Popoff had an earpiece disguised as a hearing aid which enabled him to receive "the gift of knowledge" regarding his attendees' ills—not from God but from his wife and others who had gleaned information from people as they entered an auditorium and waited for the service to begin. The scam was revealed by the lead investigator in 1986 on an episode of the *Johnny Carson Show*! As a result, 39.17 MHz is now referred to as "God's frequency."[105]

But, consummate manipulator that he is, over the last thirty-five years Popoff has managed to repackage his "ministry" several times and milk his approach for all its worth: "He gets rich, you get hope."[106] Popoff considers it a win-win situation! Yes, THERE'S ALWAYS MORE TO EVERY STORY.

From Prison to Praise

In eleventh century Germany, Ashkenazi Jews would listen to the Torah (Genesis through Deuteronomy) read in both Hebrew and Aramaic. This was necessary because even before the time of Jesus, Aramaic had replaced Hebrew as the more common language of the Jews.[107] One of the cantors (prayer leaders) among those Ashkenazi Jews, Meir ben Isaac Nehorai, wrote a liturgical poem in Aramaic which was read, sung, or chanted before the reading of the Ten Commandments on the first day of the Jewish feast of Pentecost.[108]

Laura Lieber, a professor at Duke University's Center for Jewish Studies, writes that this poem extols "God's power and majesty, God's Torah and its significance, and God's people Israel, with a recurring thematic focus on Israel's enduring loyalty to the covenant symbolized by the Torah."[109] It is considered one of Judaism's most familiar and cherished liturgical poems.[110]

Eight centuries later–in 1868–another German citizen was born. When Martin was four years old, he emigrated with his family to Iowa. Eventually he was called to Christian ministry and became a Nazarene pastor. In 1911 he and his family moved to Kansas City, where he was involved in establishing the Nazarene Publishing House.

Martin had a passion for Christian poetry and music, both penning the words and composing the melodies for hundreds of songs.[111] One of Martin's best remembered songs is "The Royal Telephone." Its chorus goes:

Telephone to glory, oh, what joy divine!
I can feel the current moving on the line,
Built by God the Father for His loved and own,
We may talk to Jesus through this royal telephone.

Prior to moving on to California, he heard an evangelist read the lines of a poem that had been found written on a wall in an insane asylum after the death of an unknown patient imprisoned there. Those words so moved Martin that he wrote them down to make sure they were preserved for posterity.[112]

The situation Martin and his family faced in California as the Great Depression approached and he experienced financial losses, forced him to take a job loading oranges and lemons into crates at a local packing plant. In the plant and back at home he began putting together what became the first two verses and chorus of a new hymn. But in those days, publishers wanted hymns with at least three verses. And try as he might, he just couldn't come up with a third one.[113]

The movie *Indescribable* is based on this part of his family's life.[114] The film does take some artistic license, suggesting that his children set themselves the task of coming up with that elusive third verse. According to the film, in one of their father's books the children found a bookmark which bore the words which Martin had copied down in that earlier evangelistic meeting. When the children pointed out those words to their father, he found they set perfectly to the music he had composed for the other verses![115]

However, before the song could be published, Martin and his children needed to see if the words of that third verse had originated with the asylum patient or with someone else, whose permission to use the words would be required. As they inquired among various sources, they found a pastor who was familiar with the words but didn't know who had written them. But he sent them to a Jewish Rabbi whom he felt might know. And sure enough, the rabbi did know who had written the words: none other than Meir ben Isaac Nehorai, whose copyright had run out over eight hundred years before![116]

And undoubtedly, Martin's best-known and most cherished hymn is the one which incorporates words from a revered Jewish poem written in Aramaic and translated into English centuries later.

And here's that elusive third verse:

> Could we with ink the ocean fill, And were the skies of parchment made;
>
> Were ev'ry stalk on earth a quill, And ev'ry man a scribe by trade;
>
> To write the love of God above Would drain the ocean dry;
>
> Nor could the scroll contain the whole Tho' stretched from sky to sky.[117]

And this third verse of Martin's—Frederick Martin Lehman's—song, "The Love of God," consists of words which have been repeated on Pentecost by Jewish people for centuries, the very day almost two thousand years ago when God sent the Holy Spirit to convict, convince, teach, empower, and comfort us.

One difference between the original poem and the version found on the wall in the insane asylum is especially noteworthy. The original emphasizes God's grandeur, the greatness of His glory, and His power, as seen in His deliverance of the Ten Commandments on Mt. Sinai.[118] But the latter celebrates the immensity of the love of God expressed in His deliverance of those who *fail* to keep the Ten Commandments:

> "While we were still sinners, Christ died for us" (*Romans* 5:8 NIV).

We can be freed from the prison of our sins and forever after lift up our praise to the One who has demonstrated His unending love for us! Yes, THERE'S ALWAYS MORE TO EVERY STORY.

Front Page

A large portion of the *Bible* consists of historical accounts. And in telling about people and events, *Scripture* provides many cultural and geographical details. Some of these details, as well as some of these people and events, are mentioned in extrabiblical records and/ or verified by archeological findings. For nearly three thousand years, the written history preserved in the *Bible* has provided a framework within which archeological findings could be understood and even anticipated.

For example, the *New Testament* describes the pool beside which Jesus healed a paralytic man, as recounted in John chapter five. According to John, this pool–the pool of Bethesda–was near the sheep gate in Jerusalem and had five colonnaded-and-covered porches. Skeptics suggested that this account was a later addition to the Gospel of John by a different writer who was unfamiliar with Jerusalem. However, in the late 1800s, archeologists discovered the pool and porches exactly as John had described them.[119]

Archeological findings can provide added context to *Bible* passages, help resolve questions about passages which are difficult to understand, and validate the reliability and truthfulness of *Scripture*. Some of the *New Testament* homes discovered in the vicinity of Capernaum had flat roofs covered with large baked tiles and accessed by an outside staircase.[120] Because of the crowd surrounding a house in Capernaum where Jesus was teaching, friends of a paralytic man who were hoping that Jesus would heal him "made a hole in the roof" and lowered their friend on his pallet in front of Jesus. Probably the hole was created by removing some of the roof tiles. If so, the roof wasn't damaged, and the owners of the house would not have been inconvenienced. But what was truly most important was that the paralytic's sins were forgiven, his handicap was healed, and Jesus demonstrated that He was truly the Messiah. (Mark 2:1-12)

Another of Jesus' miracles involved the healing of blind men near Jericho. One *Gospel* mentions only one blind man and has Jesus performing the healing as He entered the city, while two *Gospels* refer to Him healing two blind men as He left the city. These could have been separate events, with both occurring as Jesus was traveling to Jerusalem for His final Passover. But archeology has confirmed that these two accounts could have referred to the same event because there were two cities of Jericho, the old and the new. If Jesus healed the blind men between the two cities, He would have been leaving the one and entering the other. And one of the two blind men could have been spokesman for both.[121]

If skeptics question the reality of people and events mentioned in the *New Testament*, including Jesus of Nazareth and the Resurrection, they have no problem extending their skepticism into the more distant past. One common theme is that the writings of *Scripture* must have changed significantly since they were first penned. If you've ever played the game of telegraph, you know it doesn't take many whispered exchanges to alter a message. So, how likely is it that the *Bible* has not changed significantly as it's been copied and translated into different languages over several thousand years?

The Dead Sea Scrolls, found in caves in Israel in what is now Qumran National Park, hold the answer. Over a period of years beginning in 1946, the complete book of Isaiah and portions of every other book in the *Old Testament* except Esther were discovered. At the time, these were the oldest portions of *Scripture* in existence, and their discovery has resolved some difficulties faced by modern *Bible* translators.[122]

For instance, the much-disputed wording of a phrase in Psalm

22:16 translated either "like a lion they were at my hands and feet" (JPS Tanakh 1917) or "they pierced my hands and my feet" (NASB), was cleared up. A discovery made during the ongoing examination of the Dead Sea Scrolls corroborated the *second* of these translations, a statement occurring in a *Psalm* which Christians consider *prophetic of Jesus' Messiahship*—Jesus, whose hands and feet were pierced when He was crucified.[123]

But most significantly, the Dead Sea Scrolls reveal the faithfulness with which the text and meaning of *Scripture* have been preserved over millennia of copying and translation. All differences between ancient and modern versions have been found to be minor and do not affect biblical doctrines.[124]

Certainly the most heralded archeological discovery in recent years dealing with the historical accuracy of the *Bible* is the Tel Dan inscription. This inscription was found in 1993 engraved on a stone fragment buried at the site of an ancient Canaanite city. The city was located in what was once the Kingdom of Israel, the northern portion of the divided Kingdom of Solomon. Written in Old Aramaic characters, the inscription is the first nonbiblical reference ever discovered which mentions King David.

Up to this time many scholars had disputed whether David had even existed. Yet his importance as the king through whose house and lineage the King of Kings would come cannot be overstated. The inscription was probably dictated by Hazael, a Syrian king who lived over one hundred years *after* David. His reference to the "House of David" confirms David's existence and continuing significance.[125] And so extraordinarily central to the verification of the Bible's historical accuracy is this "House of David" inscription that its discovery was featured on the cover of *The New York Times*![126] Yes, THERE'S ALWAYS MORE TO EVERY STORY.

Highways of the Sea

◆◆◆◆◆

Well-worn trails, railroad tracks, and networks of roads form the transportation routes of one-fourth of Earth's land surface. Rivers also form well-defined transportation highways. And one's location along such established pathways could usually be determined by reference to physical waypoints including both natural and manmade objects. However, in times past, navigating large lakes and the world's oceans was far more difficult. Until the 1400s, travel in these waters was primarily restricted to the shorelines.

Development of the compass and various devices for measuring latitude, together with the gradual creation of increasingly accurate navigational charts, gave mariners the ability to venture farther offshore. However, measuring longitude on the ocean proved a much more daunting problem. And without knowing both a ship's latitude and longitude, her position on the open sea could not be pinpointed. It was not until around 1760 that an amateur clockmaker from England, John Harrison, produced the marine chronometer, a clock so accurate that it could be used to determine longitude.[127]

Unlike dry land, the seas are in constant motion. While atmospheric conditions such as wind and weather affect transportation on both land and sea, there are factors unique to marine navigation. These include tides, waves, currents, and other motion phenomena. Together with wind and weather they can facilitate or hinder navigation. For example, tides can bring a ship safely over a sandbar or cause it to run aground. Normal waves can help propel a ship to its destination, while rogue waves can capsize even the largest vessels. And currents can either direct a ship along its desired path or in an unfavorable direction.

The fact that winds, tides, waves, and currents affect ocean navigation have been known for thousands of years, primarily from the experiences of those navigating coastlines. But as navigational instruments allowed mariners to ply the open ocean with confidence, and charts provided increasingly accurate information about what they would find, mariners became more and more aware of the presence of additional currents and their profound influence on shipping.[128]

However, knowledge of prevailing winds and currents remained largely a patchwork that needed to be pieced together. Early on, some countries and marine shipping companies kept to themselves their accumulated knowledge of wind patterns and currents in the areas they traveled. Portugal was famous for its trade with China, and Portuguese sailors were sworn to secrecy regarding trade routes.[129]

But as more and more parts of the nautical puzzle were discovered, it remained for someone with sufficient vision, influence, perseverance, and resources to orchestrate production of a comprehensive chart of the world's wind patterns and ocean currents which would be available to *all* seafarers. Nations were anxious to obtain this knowledge not only for safety and economic reasons, but also to provide their navies with tactically useful information.[130]

The man who eventually fulfilled this vital need began his career as a U. S. Navy midshipman in 1825. On his first voyage, Matthew Maury developed an interest in investigating the seas and learning methods of navigation, an interest which was further aroused on a subsequent voyage aboard the first American warship to circle the globe, the USS Vincennes.

Eventually put in charge of the *Navy Depot of Charts and Instruments*, Maury began to organize information gleaned from ships' logs and other sources, and to solicit additional observations from seafarers everywhere. As a result of Maury's work, documented in his 1847 *Wind and Current Chart of the North Atlantic*, he became well known and respected in shipping circles throughout the world. And his book *The Physical Geography of the Sea*, published in 1855, was the first comprehensive treatise on oceanography.[131]

Maury became known as "Pathfinder of the Seas," "Father of Modern Oceanography and Naval Meteorology" and "Scientist of the Seas."[132] His foresight, persistence, and confidence in his undertaking were inspired by his childhood exposure to the *Bible* and his knack for remembering *Scripture* passages. To him, the *Psalms* were not only signposts of the Creator's care and sovereignty, but also of His very design for "the earth he has given to mankind" *(Psalm* 115:16 NIV).[133] Thus, in pursuing knowledge of the marine environment and navigation, he took literally the words of Psalm 8:6-9:

> You have given [man] dominion over the works of
> your hands; you have put all things under his feet, . . .
> the fish of the sea, [and] whatever passes along the
> paths of the seas. O LORD, our Lord, how majestic
> is your name in all the earth! (Psalm 8:6-9 ESV)[134]

Yes, THERE'S ALWAYS MORE TO EVERY STORY.

Hippocrates

—————— ◆◆◆◆◆◆ ——————

Hippocrates lived between the fifth and fourth centuries B.C. in Greece. Born shortly before Cyrus the Great of Persia began allowing Jews exiled to Babylon to return to their homeland under the leadership of Zerubbabel, Hippocrates lived sixty years into the period between the *Old* and *New Testaments*. He is known as the Father of Western Medicine for his transformation of the practice of medicine from a private, family-centered process limited to tradition-based methods of healing, to a universally applicable public system based on a growing understanding of physical causes and effects.[135] Hippocrates stated that "The medical art has to consider three factors: the disease, the patient, and the physician." Ethically, the patient was the most important of these factors. The key ethical concept of Hippocrates' philosophy of medicine was "do no harm."[136]

Although the Hippocratic Oath taken by many physicians over the centuries may not have been written by Hippocrates, it is thought to reflect the ethical expectations he had for himself and those who practiced his medical approach. Yet, as worthy as many of his ethical expectations surely are, others fail to be compatible with Christianity on a number of counts.

In the first place, the oath calls on all the Greek gods and goddesses to bear witness to the promises oath takers make. Second, it restricts the knowledge of the "art" of medicine to "those who have taken the Healer's oath." Third, it fails to recognize that for a doctor to "keep pure and holy both my life and my art," a practitioner must call on the only One who is holy. And fourth, it does not call into question the belief common in Hippocrates' time that only the healthy and physically fit had an adequate quality of life to be treated with dignity:[137]

> According to this belief, citizenship, kinship, status, merit, and virtue formed the foundation of claims to human rights or human worth. The basic human worth of orphans, slaves, foundlings, prisoners, and the physically defective was not recognized.[138]

Whatever the extent to which this classical Greek perspective limited the application of public medicine, the Judeo-Christian version that emerged was firmly rooted in the teaching that *all* persons are created in the image of God. Christians are to love all people, especially the vulnerable, with the love which flows from God to every believer.

And doing so extends to bodily needs, in spite of the false belief, known as Gnosticism, that the body is bad and only the spirit has value.[139] Christianity clearly teaches that human beings are both embodied and ensouled, and operate and have needs in both body and soul.[140] "The Christian conception of Jesus as perfect man contributed," says [Oregon State University professor of history, Gary B.] Ferngren, "to raising the body to a status that it had never enjoyed in paganism."[141]

Being made in God's image, *all* people have inherent dignity and value. And this fact was ratified fully by the incarnation and willing sacrifice of the Son of God. His image bearers are *so valued* by Him that He desires them to enjoy eternal life in His presence. Jesus is clearly *pro life*:

> This was the basis for Christian repudiation of abortion, infanticide, the gladiatorial games, and suicide.[142]

> Just as God demonstrated in the Incarnation his solidarity with those who suffer, so the members of his 'body' must demonstrate their solidarity with the suffering poor.[143]

> In sum, the image of God, especially as refracted through the prism of the Incarnation, was the basis for Christian compassion and care for those in need.[144]

The advantage of revealed truth over relativism is decisive. The *Bible* provides moral truth which applies to all people in all ages. This truth is evident in the modifications and additions which Christianity has made to the Hippocratic Oath.

On the other hand, the moral relativism evident in the philosophies of our time judges this Christian version to be prejudicial and divisive, placing roadblocks in the way of people's right to create their own morality. Most notably, the idea that humans are made in God's image is rejected, and abortion, infanticide, and assisted suicide are considered morally acceptable basic human rights.[145]

We need to remember that meeting human needs, especially the need for healing, was the heart of Jesus' ministry. He reminded His hearers that "It is not the healthy who need a doctor, but the sick" (Mark 2:17 NIV). His work recognized the need for healing of both body and soul. Restoring sight to the blind, hearing to the deaf, speech to the mute, and wholeness to the otherwise disabled were carried out side-by-side with casting out evil spirits, addressing emotional and spiritual struggles, and forgiving sin.

Above all He performed heart transplants and conquered life's greatest health challenges: the Devil, our own fallen nature, and death. Of course, He had no need for medications or surgeries in order to heal. But God did give His image bearers not only access to the physical patterns behind prevention and healing, but most importantly, the prescription for an abundant life on earth, and eternal life in His dis-ease-less Kingdom. Our Creator is truly the Great Physician and Healer. Yes, THERE'S ALWAYS MORE TO EVERY STORY.

Independence Day

+ ✦ ✦ ✦ ✦ ✦ +

The 4ᵗʰ of July is more than fireworks and family picnics. It is our nation's festival of freedom! It is Independence Day–the birthday of our nation. The roots of independence reach deep. Many of those who had made their way to the New World from the Old in the period following Columbus were fleeing religious, political, and economic oppression. Yet, as long as the new settlements remained under the domination of European powers, they would be subject to the possibility of tyranny from abroad.[146]

Britain, Spain, and Portugal were the main players in efforts to expand empires to the Americas–but all would eventually be forced to withdraw most of their American claims in the face of a rising tide of independence and more pressing problems elsewhere. What began as the pioneer independence demanded by isolation in an untamed wilderness was to ripen into the political independence demanded by the abuses inflicted by external governments and by the colonists' subsequent determination to manage their own affairs.[147] So it was that the success of the thirteen colonies in obtaining independence from Britain inspired independence movements elsewhere in the Americas, and even back in Europe.[148]

And wherever independence was achieved, the accomplishment was regularly commemorated. Of the numerous incidents comprising the struggle for independence, a single episode was commonly selected to represent the entire course of events. The long road to U.S. independence was crowded with momentous episodes–the Boston

Tea Party, the meeting of the First Continental Congress, the "shot heard round the world," Cornwallis's surrender, the ratification of the Constitution. But passage by members of the Continental Congress of a "declaration of the American position" in its conflict with Britain would ultimately be selected as the event by which citizens of the United States would memorialize their independence.[149]

The Declaration of Independence presents clearly and eloquently both the decision of the colonists to completely separate themselves from the British Empire and the reasons behind their action. In part it reads:

> We hold these truths to be self-evident, that all men are created equal, that they are endowed by their Creator with certain inalienable rights, that among these are Life, Liberty and the pursuit of Happiness.—That to secure these rights, Governments are instituted among men, deriving their just powers from the consent of the governed,— That whenever any Form of Government becomes destructive of these ends . . . [it becomes necessary to] throw off such government. . . . Such is now the necessity which constrains [these colonies]. . . . For the support of this Declaration, with a firm reliance on the Protection of Divine Providence, we mutually pledge to each other our Lives, our Fortunes, and our sacred Honor.[150]

And the regular celebration of the passage of this document is an essential means of renewing and increasing appreciation for all that our freedom comprises. The 4th of July signifies something truly worthy of being remembered by every American citizen.

Other nations have their own stories of independence won, and their own special times of celebration. Israel, for example. Now, you know that the children of Jacob/Israel were delivered from Egyptian slavery and became an independent nation. But what about the fact that in this case, contrary to similar instances of independence achieved, the celebration was held *before* the victory was won? This of course was because God had guaranteed deliverance, that He would win the victory for them. And it helps us understand that for Christians, Israeli Independence Day is a far more important occasion than even the 4th of July!

For you see, Israel's delivery from bondage and emergence as an independent nation is commemorated on the 15th of the Jewish month Nisan, the day on which the Passover meal is served, the meal from which bread and wine were selected to remind us of the One Who liberated us from the domain of Satan and made us citizens of Heaven. And of such *incomparable importance* is this deliverance that, rather than only one day a year, but "as often" as we can, we participate in Communion–the Lord's Supper–to remember the One Who freed us from sin on that ultimate Independence Day (I Corinthians 11:26 ESV)! Yes, THERE'S ALWAYS MORE TO EVERY STORY.

Inspiring Tales

+ + + + + +

Tremendous technological advances since the 1800s make it very difficult for today's public to appreciate the differences between life before the Industrial Revolution and life since. During the 1800s the Industrial Revolution brought mass production along with improvements in transportation, agriculture, and mining, all powered by steam engines. At the same time these innovations brought alterations to human behaviors and relationships.[151] For some it provided new opportunities to use time in more creative and less tedious ways, and this amid a growing struggle to implement social reforms, including economic and political equality for women.[152]

Ella Dale attended a school in New York City that focused on domestic skills, but she had an interest in writing and possessed unusual talent for it. However, the school's superintendent insisted she focus on sewing and other household subjects. And it took a visiting phrenologist's examination of her facial features to change the superintendent's mind. (Phrenology is the unsupported belief that certain mental abilities and character traits can be determined by measuring bumps on the skull.) This phrenologist reported that Ella had a unique writing talent and should be encouraged to develop it. Over time, Ella was counted on to provide and read written pieces for school events and public communication.[153]

At this same school, Lizzie Edwards demonstrated special musical talent and was allowed to study singing, learned to play the guitar, piano, and organ, and became a much-admired harpist. Her reputation led her to become the first woman to address the United States Senate, and subsequently a joint session of Congress. She spoke on behalf of disabled people, a segment of society whose fitness to contribute to the public good was not adequately recognized. Later, she became a friend of presidents and even stayed in the White House on several occasions. Once she even sang and played in the White House music room for President James K. Polk and his wife.[154]

Leah Carlton was a talented writer whose works caught the interest of multitudes, not only in the United States but throughout the world. Her husband was blind yet was a gifted pianist and composer who was Leah's greatest fan. He encouraged her writing and, moreover, set some of her words to music. Many of her writings were featured in the *Saturday Evening Post* and other prominent publications. She even wrote "hit parade" quality lyrics including "Rosalie, the Prairie Flower," which, set to music, sold thousands of copies and earned her a largely unheard-of return in royalties. And her relatives include world famous pop singers.[155]

Henrietta E. Blair showed an amazing ability to memorize and retain information. From childhood she was encouraged by her mother and grandmother to memorize *Scripture.* She could eventually quote much of the *Old* and *New Testaments* and could select passages which shed light on the many situations and circumstances which she encountered.[156] Her abilities enabled her to readily formulate and express ideas, and sometimes when dictating to a secretary, her thoughts would come together so quickly that it was impossible for the secretary to get the words down. She once wrote lyrics for a tune immediately after first hearing it, presenting them to the composer within only a few minutes. The composer left by train shortly afterwards, elated that he had a new song to present to his compatriots at the convention he was heading to![157] Among Henrietta's most noted accomplishments was authoring the words to the very first secular operetta created by Americans: *The Flower Queen.*[158]

Maud Marion dedicated her later years to the downtrodden of the Bowery District and other slum areas of New York City. She considered herself primarily a missionary and did much to alleviate the struggles of poor immigrants and citizens. She supported a number of skid road missions including the Water Street Mission, America's *first* rescue mission. She spoke to the needs of the urban poor at YMCAs, churches, and prisons, while also advocating for the women's temperance movement. And she reached out to those who wandered into any mission she was visiting, encouraging them to turn from darkness to light. [159]

Not coincidentally, all of the women named above *became blind soon after birth*. As a matter of fact, their names are among over two hundred pen names for *the same person*! For you see, the five names mentioned above are different names for a woman who produced the words of so many hymns and Gospel songs that her publishers felt their hymnbooks would be more widely received if purchasers didn't realize the same person had written so many of the hymns they contained![160]

Having fashioned the lyrics of about nine thousand hymns, hymns which were eagerly received, Fanny Crosby became known as the "Queen of Gospel Song Writers." Among those hymns are "Blessed Assurance," "To God Be the Glory," and "Tell Me the Story of Jesus." In addition, she assembled the words of over one thousand pop songs and secular poems. And those world-famous pop singers among her relatives? . . . Bing and Bob Crosby.[161] Yes, THERE'S ALWAYS MORE TO EVERY STORY.

Masks

Those of us who have lived during the COVID-19 pandemic are quite accustomed to wearing masks. But long before that event, people have worn masks, both literally and figuratively. Ancient Greek drama featured actors who wore masks, and for good reasons:

> The masks and costumes were highly stylized and exaggerated making the characters easy to identify even from a great distance. The actors with comedic roles wore thin soled shoes, while tragic actors were elevated on stage wearing thick, raised platform shoes. . . . All the actors were male, and they all played multiple roles, so a mask was used to show the change in character or mood. Masks challenged the actors to portray their characters' feelings in more subtle ways, with voice and body language, since they couldn't use facial expressions.[162]

Furthermore, these wooden, leather, or painted canvas masks acted as megaphones, making it possible for actors to be heard in the vastness of the Greek amphitheaters. The familiar frowning and smiling masks indicating tragedy and comedy have symbolized drama ever since that time.[163]

During the Middle Ages masks were used in plays designed to attract churchgoers who had tired of the usual church format and didn't understand the Latin used throughout church services. These so-called Mystery Plays dramatized *Bible* stories, the lives of Saints, and moral choices:[164]

> In plays dramatizing portions of the Bible, grotesques of all sorts, such as devils, demons, dragons, and personifications of the seven deadly sins, were brought to stage life by the use of masks.[165]

Some cultures believe that masks contain a "spirit force" which interacts with its wearer:

> [T]he performer loses his previous identity and assumes a new one. Upon donning the mask, the wearer sometimes undergoes a psychic change and as in a trance assumes the spirit character depicted by the mask. . . . He seems to become an automaton, without his own will, which has become subservient to that of the personage of the mask.[166]

In Western Culture, by the twentieth century, masks were no longer a common feature in plays. Performers were able to use their faces to help portray characters without the limitations imposed by masks. Of the several different acting techniques which were developed at the time, one is eerily similar to the belief that mask and actor blend their spiritual powers so that the actor not only "becomes" the character they're portraying but may be changed themself by the experience. "Method acting" is defined as:

> a technique or type of acting in which an actor aspires to encourage sincere and emotionally expressive performances by fully inhabiting the role of the character. It is an emotion-oriented

technique instead of classical acting that is primarily action-based.[167]

Marlon Brando, of *On the Waterfront* fame, is considered the consummate method actor. To prepare for a part in one film:

> Brando stayed in a hospital bed for an entire month to get in the mindset for the injured veteran he'd be playing. In Brando's best films, he doesn't seem to be acting at all but embodying the character.[168]

But method acting can take a toll. Realistically expressing the emotions of a character requires an actor to dredge up his own emotional experiences, and if these personal experiences have never been resolved, they can be in for trouble. Sleep deprivation, personality changes, and psychotic episodes can result.[169]

And of course, these and other negative effects are experienced as well by people in all walks of life. After all, we each "wear masks" at times. Usually not the theatrical type, but a spiritual and psychological projection of ourselves which is not true to reality. For whatever reasons, we are compelled to hide our real identities. Whether our masks are idealized or self-disparaging versions of ourselves, they have an influence on our lives. For example, we may appear egocentric or withdrawn, narcissistic or suicidal. Few indeed may be the people with whom we can be mask-free without fearing they will put us down or condemn us.[170]

By contrast, we are told that, beginning with his encounter with God on Mt. Sinai, each time Moses told his fellow Israelites what God had commanded during his personal conversations with Him, the light of glory shone from his face (Exodus 34:29-35). But because of their record of rebelliousness, Moses would then put on a literal mask–a veil–"to conceal the temporary glory of the Old Covenant."[171] Although this glory faded, Jesus' death has completely eliminated the need for a veil, so that:

we all, who with unveiled faces contemplate the
Lord's glory, are being transformed into his image
with ever-increasing glory, which comes from the
Lord, who is the Spirit (II Corinthians 3:18 NIV).

When Jesus died, the massive veil which separated the Holy
of Holies from the rest of the Temple "was torn in two from top
to bottom," giving Christians direct access to God's presence
(Mark:15:38 NASB). We can now become what God intended us
to be all along: His adopted children, who, because we are being
transformed into the image of His Son, are no longer compelled to
wear masks! Yes, THERE'S ALWAYS MORE TO EVERY STORY.

Metamorphosis

———— ✦✦✦✦✦ ————

The word "metamorphosis" comes from a Greek word consisting of two main parts: "meta," meaning "change" or "after," and "morph," meaning "form." Thus, "metamorphosis" means *transformation*.[172] While humans and some animals, including the higher vertebrates, develop *directly* from embryo to adult by increasing in size and acquiring mature functions, others develop *indirectly* by passing through one or more intermediate stages which differ from the adult in both appearance and behavior.[173]

The process of indirect development is known as *biological metamorphosis*. A frog egg hatches into a tadpole which eventually transforms into an adult frog. A butterfly egg yields a caterpillar which fattens up, then transforms into a pupa in which the caterpillar's tissues are rearranged so that what emerges is a colorful flying adult.[174] And biological metamorphosis can exhibit more complex and bizarre features than do these more straight-forward types.

Take the immortal jellyfish, for example. Its eggs hatch into free-swimming larvae which eventually become polyps resembling sea anemones and attach to solid surfaces on the sea floor. These polyps in turn transform into adult jellyfish. But if environmental conditions threaten their survival, these jellyfish can again become polyps and await more favorable conditions to be born again as adult jellyfish![175] Yet, whether they undergo metamorphosis or direct development, all living things eventually dissolve into dust.

Speaking more generally, metamorphosis is defined as "a change of the form or nature of a thing or person into a completely different one, by natural or supernatural means."[176] Geological changes produced by shifts of the earth's crustal plates, erosion, and other processes, resculpt our planet's surface. Meanwhile, as the sun provides us with light and heat, it's also running out of fuel. And according to physicists, the sun's death throes will ultimately incinerate the earth![177]

According to the Big Bang Theory, our universe began when a tiny packet of matter and energy blew up, sending its treasure of subatomic particles and raw energy in all directions. According to some estimates, this event occurred 13.8 billion years ago and has resulted in the evolution of the universe into the form we observe today. And the vastness of the energy released during the Big Bang is suggested by the discovery that the most distant galaxies are moving outward into the void at a *still increasing* rate! Furthermore, this void into which the universe is expanding is *uncharted territory*.[178]

The broader definition of metamorphosis quoted above mentions the possibility of *spiritual means* of bringing about change in, transformation of, the form or nature of persons. Within the first three chapters of Genesis, we find that human beings have both a physical and spiritual nature, are created in the image of God (share in a limited sense some of His attributes), have been tasked by Him to reproduce their kind and develop culture, and are accountable to accept the restraints He places on us for our own well-being.

But we also find that we're vulnerable to the counsel of a created spirit-being who, as a result of his own free choice, transformed himself– *metamorphosed*–from chief archangel to chief archenemy of God:

> How you are fallen from heaven, O Lucifer, son of the morning! *How* you are cut down to the ground, [y]ou who weakened the nations! (Isaiah 14:12 NKJV).

As a result of Adam and Eve's subsequent rebellion, and ours, we too are fallen. But more importantly, we have the opportunity to be transformed–*metamorphosed*–"conformed to the image of His Son so that Jesus would be the firstborn of a new family of believers, all brothers and sisters" (Romans 8:29 VOICE).

According to atheistic materialists, there has always been something, never nothing. Therefore, there must have been something physical which preexisted the tiny something that, according to the Big Bang, accounts for our present universe.[179] But they have no answer to an important question: "Why should there be anything material in the first place?" Christianity offers the simplest explanation. There *was* nothing material in the first place; instead:

> In the beginning was the Word, and the Word was
> with God, and the Word was God. . . . Through
> him all things were made; without him nothing was
> made that has been made. (John 1:1 and 3 NIV),

Thus, God *spoke* creation, including ourselves, into existence. And at Christmas we celebrate the fact that "The Word became flesh and made his dwelling among us" (John 1:14 NIV).

The most incredible metamorphosis that has ever occurred, the greatest transformation that has ever taken place, is not something limited to the material sphere, nor even the metamorphosis of human beings into eternal images of Jesus in the perfect world to come. No, it is a metamorphosis utterly beyond human comprehension, even when our understanding is aided by the Holy Spirit. For it was the *metamorphosis* of the uncreated, self-existent, unbounded, "ground" of all being into a man, Jesus the Christ, who was both fully human and fully God, both the Son of Man and the Son of God, who would ultimately die to make eternal life available to those who humble themselves before Him! Yes, THERE'S ALWAYS MORE TO EVERY STORY!

Mr. Basketball

———— ✦✦✦✦✦ ————

It has only been around since 1891, but today, multimillion-dollar contracts and worldwide fame are earned by a chosen few who excel at basketball. Given the pervasiveness of sports in American culture, many of these professional players' names are recognized by a large portion of our population, and not a few sports buffs can provide detailed information about players' accomplishments. And each year there are efforts to identify and rank the greatest basketball players of all time.

After its creation, basketball became so popular that it didn't take many years for it to become an intercollegiate sport, with the first national championship game being played in 1922. By 1935 basketball had become a professional sport as well, eventually leading to the formation of the National Basketball Association (NBA) in 1949. Not surprisingly, most professional players emerge from the college ranks.[180] Yet some of the best-known players, including LeBron James, Kobe Bryant, and Moses Malone became professionals without any college experience.[181]

But regarding colleges, the University of Kansas has become one of the elite of the elite, basketball-wise. As of this writing Kansas has won more consecutive home games and participated in "March Madness" more often than any other team, winning three NCAA Championships.[182] One of its players is considered by some to be the first internationally recognized basketball megastar, having had outstanding college and professional careers–Wilt (The Stilt)

77

Chamberlain. In his first college game, Chamberlain scored 50 points; while in the NBA he scored 50 or more points in 118 games (Michael Jordan has the next most—31 games); and Chamberlain is the only pro ever to score 100 points in a game![183] Consider too that four of the eight basketball coaches Kansas has had to date have been inducted into the Basketball Hall of Fame.[184]

One Kansas coach initially served as the school's chapel director and taught physical education. He had previously earned an MD, and while at Kansas he used his medical knowledge to involve students in researching athletic development and the prevention and treatment of injuries. It was several years later that he was asked to coach the Kansas basketball team as well.[185]

Growing up he had excelled at sports including football, rugby, lacrosse, soccer, and gymnastics. Eventually he graduated from college with a degree in physical education, then attended a Presbyterian school which prepared students for Christian ministry, earning a degree in theology.[186] Like Fred Rogers ("Mr. Rogers" of TV fame), who was ordained by the United Presbyterian Church, not as a church pastor, but as a minister to children and their families through television, this Kansas coach chose a different route of ministry.[187]

Although a top theological student, he felt that God was *not* calling him to be a pastor or professor of theology but rather to help young men apply Christian principles in the field of physical education and sports. He viewed "fitness" as both a physical and spiritual pursuit.[188] Although his tenure as the Kansas basketball coach was relatively short, he continued to work for the university, serving also as athletic director and campus physician in addition to teaching. When he retired, he had served with the Jayhawks for nearly forty years.[189]

Like any game, basketball has undergone changes over the years. Originally conceived as an indoor game designed to meet the recreational needs of students between fall football and spring track-and-field, basketball was intended to reduce rough play and emphasize finesse. Its inventor, James Naismith, did not at first think his game even required coaching, just a clear-cut set of rules. Nor did he really approve of overemphasis on winning in what he conceived of as an enjoyable way to keep fit. He objected to the distractions–distractions from the most important aspects of life–caused by the extremes of hype, ego, and money-making which overemphasis of any sports activity can produce.[190] Yet when he attended the first Olympics which included basketball, he was overjoyed to realize that his game was being played all over the world![191]

By the way, that multitasking Kansas basketball coach who was everything from chaplain to physical education instructor to physician at the school, is also the only Jayhawk basketball coach to lose more games than he won, in spite of the fact that he invented the game![192] Yes, THERE'S ALWAYS MORE TO EVERY STORY.

Not of This Earth

——— ✦✦✦✦✦ ———

There is documentary evidence that at least two thousand years ago people were speculating about the existence of extraterrestrial life. Greeks of that time discussed the possibility of life on other planets, and around 200 A.D. a Turkish writer named Lucian penned a novel about life on the moon and sun.[193] Copernicus's conclusion that the sun is the center around which the planets revolve, published in 1543, further spurred speculation about the possibility of life on other planets.[194] In 1686, Bernard le Bovier de Fontenelle promoted interest in the possibility of extraterrestrial life in a book called *Conversations on the Plurality of Worlds*.[195]

Intelligent aliens proliferate throughout science fiction. Some are pictured remotely monitoring Earth, with either benevolent (as in *The Day the Earth Stood Still*) or malevolent (*Independence Day*) intent. Aliens, such as the creature in *It Came from Outer Space,* are depicted with the ability to shapeshift in order to interact with humans. Others, such as the pod people in *Invasion of the Body Snatchers,* simply take over the bodies of humans. Extraterrestrials are imagined communicating with humans via ESP (as in *Starship Troopers*), utilizing alien technology (*War of the Worlds*), ushering in a utopian vision (*Childhood's End*), existing in non-material form (*Color Out of Space*), defeatable if malevolent (*Dr. Who*), already living among us (*Men in Black*), and in many cases altering human history for better (*Close Encounters of the Third Kind*) or worse (*Ender's Game*).

While some people are convinced that extraterrestrials have visited Earth (perhaps even seeding it with life), and there is continuing controversy regarding the existence of UFOs, the scientific world does *not* acknowledge a first contact with extraterrestrial life. The search for extraterrestrial intelligence, SETI, traces back to early attempts to initiate communication with extraterrestrial intelligence. Initial efforts focused on visual methods, but radio signals have proved superior in penetrating deep space.[196]

From 1960 on, until its demise in 2020, the world's largest radio telescope, located in Arecibo, Puerto Rico, had been probing the skies for messages from alien intelligences. In 1974 the first radio message from Earth was sent toward the stars inviting any such intelligence to respond.[197] Unmanned spacecraft on exploratory voyages have also carried similar messages.[198] And further spurring the search has been the recent discovery of planetary systems beyond our own.[199] But, contrary to what has been depicted in multiple works of science fiction, there has *never been* any response to our efforts to communicate with extraterrestrials.

Now, in spite of the fact that notable science fiction has been produced by Christian writers such as C.S. Lewis (check out his *Space Trilogy*[200]), some science fiction aficionados contend that Christians are limited in their ability to write science fiction by the constraints of their biblical worldview. But aren't all authors constrained by their particular worldviews? Certainly, authors of science fiction who reject a biblical worldview are free to promote any of a variety of opposing worldviews.[201] Consequently, writers of science fiction often create scenarios which demean Christianity, especially God's alleged failure to practice His own moral restraints. In Arthur C. Clarke's short story "The Star," for example, the star of Bethlehem is identified as a supernova which destroyed the intelligent and peace-loving beings on a planet which revolved around it.[202]

But wait! Is it really true that earthlings have never been in contact with extraterrestrials? Although writers of science fiction are paid to *imagine* that we have made first contact, and secular scientists are paid to acknowledge that *we haven't*, what does the *Bible* have to say? A closer examination of its content reveals that the *Bible actually documents* the existence of extraterrestrial intelligences among whom *all of the abilities and objectives* portrayed in the science fiction tales noted above—from monitoring Earth to shapeshifting to altering human history—can be found! And who exactly are these extraterrestrial beings? . . . The angels! Yes, THERE'S ALWAYS MORE TO EVERY STORY.

Purpose Firm

When Bill Borden was seven, his mother, who had recently become a Christian, took him to hear famous evangelist and pastor R. A. Torrey at what would later become Moody Church in Chicago. There Borden realized that he was being offered the opportunity of a lifetime and opened his heart to God's purpose for his life. From that point on he was focused on prayer and *Bible* study and encouraging others to present their hearts to God as well.[203]

As a high school graduation gift, his very wealthy family gave him a trip around the world, resulting in his gaining first-hand knowledge of the desperate needs of many people in Asia, the Middle East, and Europe. He wrote home about his experience and expressed a desire to become a missionary. One of Borden's friends responded that Borden would be "throwing himself away as a missionary."[204]

Nevertheless, another sermon, again preached by R. A. Torrey, but this time in England, sealed Borden's determination to become a missionary no matter the cost.[205] "A story often associated with Borden says that, in response [to those who urged him to consider a career in the business world], he wrote two words in the back of his Bible: 'No reserves'": His purpose was firm and he would leave nothing to fall back on, no Plan B![206]

Reluctantly, his parents accepted their son's decision but insisted that he obtain a college education before he went to a foreign mission field.[207] Of course, the Borden name had become widely known over the nearly fifty years that had passed since entrepreneur Gail

Borden had invented a commercially viable way to condense milk by removing 60% of its water content. This process greatly increased the life of dairy products, enabling them to be shipped long distances, while at the same time making millionaires of the Bordens.[208] And entering Yale from a very wealthy family, some of his fellow scholars assumed that Bill Borden was an heir to the dairy fortune. However,

> Borden's father had made a fortune in Colorado silver mining, [and] the family was not related to the Borden Condensed Milk Company—an advantage for Borden since if asked about his wealth, he could honestly reply that his family was often mistaken for "the rich Condensed Milk firm that bears the name of Borden."[209]

> Even though young Borden was wealthy, he arrived on the campus of Yale University in 1905 trying to look like just one more freshman. Very quickly, however, Borden's classmates noticed something unusual about him and it wasn't that he had lots of money. One of them wrote: "He came to college far ahead, spiritually, of any of us. He had already given his heart in full surrender to Christ and had really done it. We who were his classmates learned to lean on him and find in him a strength that was solid as a rock, just because of this settled purpose and consecration."[210]

[During Borden's first semester,] . . . the university president spoke in a convocation about the students' need of "having a fixed purpose." After that speech, Borden wrote: "He neglected to say what our purpose should be, and where we should get the ability to persevere and the strength to resist temptations." Surveying the Yale faculty and much of the student body, Borden lamented what he saw as the end result of an empty, humanistic philosophy: moral weakness and sin-ruined lives.[211]

Subsequently, Borden and a classmate began meeting together every morning before breakfast, noting promises from the *Bible* and praying. In short order, others began to join them. As Borden's senior year began, one thousand of Yale's thirteen hundred students were meeting in groups each week for *Bible* study and prayer![212]

Meanwhile Borden threw himself into outreach beyond the campus, ministering to the needs of widows, orphans, disabled, and down and out. He established the Yale Hope Mission and personally sought out the incorrigible and discarded:[213]

> One well-traveled English visitor, when asked what had most impressed him about America, is said to have replied, "The sight of that young millionaire kneeling with his arm around a 'bum' in the Yale Hope Mission."[214]

After graduating from Yale, Borden received some lucrative job offers but turned them down, writing in his *Bible*: "No retreats."[215] He went on to do graduate work at Princeton Seminary, then set sail for China, where he hoped to share the Gospel with Uyghur [We'-gur] Muslims in northwestern China (the same group that the Communist Chinese are subjecting to genocide today!).[216] On the way, he stopped in Cairo, Egypt, to study Arabic and try to determine how to conduct outreach to Muslims. There in Cairo, 25-year-old Bill Borden contracted spinal meningitis and was called to his heavenly Father.[217]

In this context a verse in Hosea seems fitting: "I loved him, and out of Egypt I called my son" (Hosea 11:1 NIV). Historically, this passage refers to Israel's deliverance from slavery in Egypt; but prophetically it anticipates Jesus' return from Egypt after Joseph and Mary had taken Him there to escape from Herod (Matthew 2:15). And as one of God's beloved adopted sons, Bill Borden was called home from Egypt, having completed the work to which God had called him. Allegedly, a third declaration had been added to Borden's *Bible* before his death: "No regrets." In any case his legacy is surely summed up in those three phrases: "No reserves, No retreats, No regrets."[218] Yes, THERE'S ALWAYS MORE TO EVERY STORY.

Resurrection

The identity of the world's oldest living inhabitant is a subject of interest to both scientists and laymen alike. Back in his day, Methuselah reputedly became the world's oldest living person. But even then, there may have been other living things, including animals and plants, that were already older than he was. In more recent times, the redwood tree has been surpassed by the bristlecone pine as leading contender. However, further studies have suggested that the Antarctic glass sponge, an animal, may live up to 15,000 years; and a "forest" of trees "cloned" naturally from a single quaking aspen seed may be up to 80,000 years old! Nevertheless, the oldest "precisely measured" living organism to grace this planet remains the bristlecone pine, the oldest of which has been dated at over 5000 years.[219]

Another question of interest is: "Which species of living thing which still survives on Earth has been around the longest"? Without getting bogged down in such a complex issue, let's just consider one category: the oldest fruit tree which continues to thrive today. Some have suggested it is the date palm.[220] As early as the book of Genesis, the *Bible* refers to the importance of the palm tree, the translation of the word *tamar*, a word also used to refer to a beautiful woman. [221] And a woman named Tamar bore a son to Judah and is thus in the lineage of Jesus Christ, the Messiah (*Genesis* 38).

The date palm provided for basic needs of people throughout the lands of the *Bible*:

> The Jews ate the palm tree dates; the tree juices were fermented into wine; the trunk of the palm tree was used as construction timber; and the palm leaves [had medicinal properties and] were woven into baskets, mats, brooms, beds, ropes and made into furniture.[222]

When the Israelites were delivered from slavery in Egypt, they were promised that they would become residents of "a land flowing with milk and honey" (Exodus 3:17 NIV). The rabbis note that the quality of food production is highest when the soil is the most fertile. Good soil will thus allow milk and honey to "flow." The milk referred to came primarily from contented goats, "the little man's cow." And the honey was date honey![223]

Dates were cultivated commercially in the regions of "Jericho, the Dead Sea, and Jordan Valley from the fifth century BCE onward, benefitting from an optimal oasis agriculture environment of freshwater sources and subtropical climate."[224] And date palms were carved on the walls of the Temple which Solomon built, and on the walls and doors of the Temple in Ezekiel's prophetic vision.[225]

The date palm was important not only to the ancient Jews but to the empires of Greece and Rome as well. This is reflected in the appearance of date palms on Greek and Roman coins and architectural motifs. "The Greeks were reported to have carved their magnificent fluted columns of marble to memorialize the shape of the trunk of a palm tree. . . . [In addition,] [a]ncient civilizations revered palm trees as symbols of fertility, peace, and victory."[226]

The fronds (branches) of palms were used to build shelters during the Jewish Feast of Tabernacles, commemorating God's provision for Israel's forty years in the wilderness, including life-sustaining water. It was during a later celebration of this feast that Jesus proclaimed: "If anyone thirsts, let him come to me and drink. He who believes in Me, as the Scripture has said, out of his heart will flow rivers of living water" (*John* 7:37–39 NKJ). And as Jesus rode to Jerusalem prior to His crucifixion, the crowds threw palm fronds on the road before him and waved them like flags, anticipating that He would deliver them from Roman rule (John 12:12 and 13; Matthew 21:8).[227]

A third question which may catch our interest is: "What is the oldest plant seed ever to have been successfully germinated and grown to maturity"? According to the *Guinness Book of World Records*, it is a date palm seed found in Herod the Great's fortress retreat on top of a plateau near the Dead Sea. The fortress retreat's name? . . . Masada! This date palm seed was determined to be about two thousand years old!

Sprouted in 2005, it turned out to be a male tree and was named Methuselah.[228] Five years later a seed was germinated which turned out to be a female and was named Hannah. Their marriage resulted in the birth of around one hundred dates in September of 2020. Those who were privileged to savor them reported:

> They are similar in taste and form to the modern day zahidi dates. They are drier and sweeter than the medjool date and taste like natural honey.[229]

And it was not missed that the origin of these date seeds corresponds to the time of Jesus crucifixion and the destruction of the nation of Israel. Hanna was found at Qumran, site of the Dead Sea Scrolls. These ancient scrolls confirm that the original text of the *Bible* has been meticulously maintained throughout the millennia. And Masada, where Methuselah was found, was the site of the last stand of Jewish zealots against the Romans, who were determined to extinguish the Jewish nation.[230]

Orthodox Jews point to the miracle of the date seeds as a sign of the resurrection of the nation of Israel in modern times. And to orthodox Christians, the miracle of the date seeds clearly reaffirms the promise of resurrection from the dead.[231] Jesus said, "I tell you the truth, unless a kernel of wheat is planted in the soil and dies, it remains alone. But its death will produce many new kernels—a plentiful harvest of new lives" (John 12:24 NLT). Yes, THERE'S ALWAYS MORE TO EVERY STORY!

Reverse English

Complex language is one of our most distinguishing human characteristics. If you're a crossword buff you can't help but be amazed at the way English words and phrases can tightly interlock throughout a crossword puzzle–puzzle after puzzle. Accomplished crossword writers and solvers are known as cruciverbalists (cross-word-ists).[232] The seemingly limitless number of these puzzles is possible for two reasons. The first is that English words are composed from a set of 26 letters. For instance, there are over 4,000 possible 3-letter combinations containing one vowel. The second is that there are a tremendous number of English words. And words enable us to think, communicate with others, and express our thoughts in creative ways. *Words have meaning.* Consequently, the more words available, the more refined and precise our communication can be.

The variety of meanings which can be expressed through words is mind-boggling. Words can convey feelings as well as information. And the thoughts they convey can be serious or playful, reasonable or senseless, truthful or deceptive, humorous or disturbing–and are often a mixture of more than one these characteristics.

In school we learn to analyze and expand our use of language, and to determine whether words are being used literally or figuratively. Language used literally means exactly what it says: Redwood trees grow tall; language used figuratively describes something by making comparisons: Redwood trees are the skyscrapers of the forest. Our thoughts, conversations, and writings typically contain both types of language. (Any English teachers or students out there?) Comparing redwood trees to skyscrapers is an example of the figure of speech known as a metaphor. Anthropomorphism (human-form-ism) is a metaphor in which the comparison involves assigning distinctively human traits, such as complex language, to non-human beings and things.

Anthropomorphism is foundational to cartoons. Kids love cartoons and watch everything from sea sponges to vegetables engage in conversation as they cavort across the screen, doing the impossible. A pesky talking "wabbit" finds hilarious ways to pester a hapless cartoon human, and cartoon characters interact with live actors. One squeaky-voiced mouse turned in his steamboat captain's credentials and changed his name in order to help Walt Disney launch the most successful and diverse entertainment business of its kind.[233] And all of Disney's cartoons feature animals or other non-human beings and things which have human characteristics.

Interestingly, the term anthropomorphism was initially used in a theological context. Christian leaders had recognized the danger of reducing God to a super-man.[234] Even those of us who are Christians may tend to think of God as a smarter, wiser, more powerful, older version of ourselves. There is a real danger that such *human characteristics* can thereby come to define God.

Remember, Eve was led to believe that time, experience, and the knowledge of good and evil would enable her to become like God. And Adam chose to follow her example in spite of his misgivings. Ever since, many have decided to leave God out of the equation completely. Thus, man elevates himself to the status of God, then denies that God even exists! In all other cases of anthropomorphism, characteristics of a *higher order (human beings)* are assigned to members of a *lower order (non-human created beings and things)*. But in this case, it's as if God has been reduced to the status of an imaginary *Marvel Comic* superhero so that we humans can pursue our sinful ambition to displace Him!

Yet, God is *not* a figmentary super-man. He is *not* a created being, although, as Jesus, a body was created for Him:

> Therefore, when Christ enters into the world, He says, "Sacrifice and offering You have not desired, But [instead] You have prepared a body for Me [to offer]" (Hebrews 10:5 AMP).

Thus Jesus is uniquely "fully man and fully God." And God is *not* a part of creation. Instead, He is the One Who not only *created* all the patterns, stars, planets, bodies, and souls, but also *maintains* them moment-by-moment:

> The Son is the image of the invisible God, the firstborn over all creation. For in him all things were created: things in heaven and on earth, visible and invisible, whether thrones or powers or rulers or authorities; all things have been created through him and for him. He is before all things, and in him all things hold together (Colossians 1:15-17 NIV).

God is totally and eternally self-sufficient—"I Am Who I Am"— while we are totally dependent on Him (Exodus 3:14 NIV). His "otherness" is incomparable. Although our bodies resemble those of animals, we are nonetheless *more than* animals because God has made us *in His image*. And because God is spirit, this "*more than*" aspect of human nature is spiritual, not physical.

Thus, we are like Him because we each have a spirit which He has endowed with some of *His* very own attributes "to at least some degree," including intelligence, language, creativity, love, holiness, immortality, freedom, dominion, and authority.[235] And as embodied beings, we express these attributes through our bodies. All in all, we are enough like God that we can communicate with Him and choose to have an eternal relationship with Him, made possible as we are conformed to the image of Jesus (Romans 8:29). But we will never *be* God!

Incredibly, although God is completely other, in an amazing reversal of roles—the *higher order* actually *becoming* a member of the *lower order*—"He humbled Himself" and became one of us (Philippians 2:1-8 NIV). He did not merely *act like* a human, He *became* a human; not to displace us, as we seek to displace Him, but to *perfect His image in us* and enable us to join Him in His eternal Kingdom. Yes, THERE'S ALWAYS MORE TO EVERY STORY.

Science and Theology

<hr>

After Christianity was declared legal throughout the Roman Empire by Constantine the Great in 313 AD, two versions of Christian doctrine regarding the Trinity vied for acceptance.[236] One held that Jesus was a creation of God, and though without sin, was not deity. This version is known as Arianism. The other version held that Jesus is fully God, one of the three Persons who compose the one true God, and that at the Incarnation He was made fully man as well. This position is called Trinitarianism. In Rome, both understandings of the nature of God held sway at different times.[237]

The differences between these positions stem primarily from two facts: that the word *Trinity* does not appear in the *Bible* and that knowledge of the correct position results from comparing relevant passages *of Scripture* and properly deciphering their meanings through the guidance of the Holy Spirit.

One theologian wrote widely on different biblical subjects, but particularly focused on the scriptural evidence for the Trinity. And he was no slouch at meticulously exegeting *Scripture* and examining relevant extrabiblical writings, including those of the early church fathers. Some of his conclusions regarding the Trinity and future fulfillment of prophesy were definitely questionable. But there is ample evidence that he held to a thoroughly theistic worldview.[238] In his own words:

> This most beautiful system of the sun, planets, and comets, could only proceed from the counsel and dominion of an intelligent and powerful Being. . . . This Being governs all things, not as the soul of the world, but as Lord over all; and on account of his dominion he is wont to be called Lord God."
>
> The true God is a living, intelligent and powerful Being. . . . He governs all things, and knows all things that are or can be done."[239]

This multitalented gentleman's interest in alchemy, especially the effort to convert less valuable metals such as iron into more valuable metals such as gold, led him to conduct research in this area for many years. But he never did discover how to make such conversions.[240] However, the knowledge of metallurgy which he acquired during his alchemical research uniquely qualified him to become Master of England's Royal Mint.[241]

At that time, coins were made of silver and gold and not precisely milled by machines. Consequently, their uneven edges could be clipped off, melted down, and used to produce counterfeit coins, or sold as gold or silver bars, while the original coins retained their face-value. This practice was so common that it had upset the state of the British economy.

In his position at the Mint, this Renaissance man introduced procedures which made coins impossible to be clipped without losing their face-value, and had them embellished with designs that were extremely difficult to counterfeit. And in another demonstration of his virtuosity, he became a master detective, tracking down counterfeiters and seeing them prosecuted.[242] Many of his writings deal with his thirty years at the Mint.[243]

Most of his other writings reveal another aspect of his wide-ranging talents: his interest in math and science. His undergraduate years at university emphasized course work along classical lines, but on his own he pursued other scholarly interests as well, including mathematics. He went on to discover the universal law of gravitation, the three laws of motion underlying physics, optical phenomena including the color spectrum, and the advanced mathematical technique known as calculus.[244] And in addition to superior coinage, his inventions included the reflecting telescope[245] and a mouse-powered miniature windmill![246]

His magnum opus was a book titled *Mathematical Principles of Natural Philosophy* (*Principia*, for short). In it he detailed his laws of motion, universal gravitation, and planetary motion.[247] Physicist Stephen Hawking and many other scientists of modern times consider *Principia* the greatest science book ever written.[248] Poet Alexander Pope paid tribute to its author in an evocative couplet:

> Nature and nature's laws lay hid in night; God said,
> "Let Newton be," and all was light.[249]

Though he was born prematurely and not expected to survive,[250] Isaac Newton went on to usher in the age of empirical science, serve as President of the Royal Society (equivalent to the National Academy of Sciences in the US), and be knighted by England's Queen Anne.[251]

And Newton himself felt that the two years the university he attended–Cambridge–was closed due to the ravages of a pandemic (bubonic plague), requiring him to isolate at home (à la COVID-19), were the most productive of his scientific and mathematical career![252] Yes, THERE'S ALWAYS MORE TO EVERY STORY.

Shell Game

++++++

"Blessed are you when people insult you and persecute you, and falsely say all kinds of evil against you because of Me. Rejoice and be glad, for your reward in heaven is great; for in the same way they persecuted the prophets who were before you" (Matthew 5:11 and 12 NASB 1995).

In 1937, on a site in the Eastern foothills of the Andes Mountains, the Shell Oil Company established a base of operations for oil exploration in the jungle to the east. The base included an airstrip and a few buildings. This was the beginning of the town of Shell, Ecuador. Due to several attacks by jungle tribes, failure to discover any oil reserves, and the growing importance of Middle Eastern oil, Shell Oil abandoned the town in 1948.[253] The next year, Mission Aviation Fellowship set up an operations center in Shell to support missionary work in Ecuador. In the early 1950's, missionaries at Shell launched "Operation Auca," an effort to develop peaceful relations with, and present the Gospel to, an unreached indigenous tribe—the Aucas.[254]

After an Auca village had been located by air, Missionary pilot Nate Saint flew his airplane in a tight spiral near the village in order to lower gifts to the natives in a bucket tied to the plane. He did this over a period of weeks, and the natives eventually reciprocated by placing gifts for their visitors into the bucket. Although the Aucas were feared for their willingness to kill their own tribespeople as well as outsiders, Saint and four of his fellow missionaries—Jim Elliot,

Pete Fleming, Roger Youderian, and Ed McCully–felt their efforts had set the stage for face-to-face meetings.

Landing on a beach at the edge of the river near the village, their initial meeting was friendly. But unknown to them, in order to deflect the anger of fellow Aucas, a tribesman who had violated tribal law accused the missionaries of attacking him. The next day, members of the tribe killed all five of the missionaries.[255]

The story of their martyrdom touched hearts around the world and was featured in a *Life Magazine* cover story and in other publications, including *Reader's Digest*. The event also inspired many young Christians to pursue missionary work in far-flung parts of the Earth.[256]

A year before the killings, Rachel Saint, Nate's sister, had begun learning the Auca language by working with Dayuma, an Auca woman who had left her home territory when her life was endangered. Dayuma was the first of her tribe to become a Christian.[257] And since *Auca* means *enemy* or *rebel*, Rachel chose to identify the tribe by the name they have for themselves: *Waorani* or *Huaorani* (Wow-ran´-ē´), meaning "they are true people." She recognized that the Waorani were made in the image of God and were equal in value to any other people.[258]

In 1958, Dayuma led Rachel Saint, Elisabeth Elliot, and Elisabeth's three-year-old daughter Valerie to a Waorani village where they continued to learn the language, developed a peaceful relationship with the villagers, had Dayuma preach the Gospel, and saw some saved. One result of their ministry was that the number of homicides in the tribe dropped almost ninety percent.[259]

While many anthropologists teach that attacks by Waorani warriors were conducted merely to protect themselves and their rain forest habitat from outside intruders:

> The Huaorani themselves speak rather unemotionally, or casually, about the high cost that their fierce autonomy had brought, with

around six out of every ten deaths being murders, long before the missionaries appeared. Many of the Huaorani themselves estimated that they were killing themselves toward extinction before the missionaries helped them see benefit in stopping the killing.[260]

But in 1967, prospecting for oil in the Ecuadorian jungle was allowed to begin anew, this time by the Texaco Oil Company, because the government was looking for new sources of income.[261] However, the threat of unreached Waorani endangering oil field workers still needed to be addressed. Since the efforts of the missionaries to evangelize the Waorani were widely seen as an effective means of pacifying and civilizing them, the oil interests and the Ecuadorian government urged the missionaries to speed up their work.

As a result, those who opposed missionary work jumped to the conclusion that the missionaries were scheming with the oil interests and Ecuadorian government in order to achieve their separate agendas.[262] According to these opponents:

> Using aircraft supplied by Texaco, missionaries searched for Huaorani homes, and pressured and tricked Huaorani clans into leaving areas where the oil company wanted to work. More than 200 Huaorani were contacted and physically removed from the path of the oil crews, and taken to live in a distant Christian settlement.[263]

One of the two women who completed the translation of the *New Testament* into the Waorani language–Wao–stated that Christian "missionaries are normal people, . . . an imperfect, failing lot" who are "motivated to make [Jesus Christ] known to those in need."[264] And doing so demands that they *must not* coerce, pressure, or trick people into anything. Nor must they "physically remove" people against their will. The truth is that the Waorani *themselves* saw the missionary efforts to alter their way of life as an opportunity to live in peace and prevent tribal self-extinction.[265]

Rachel Saint, Dayuma, and Elizabeth Elliot established a camp in Wao territory in 1958, and over the next ten years Waorani from various locations joined the peaceful community. But in 1969, the government of Ecuador approved the creation of an "official Waorani reservation" to which "pacified" Waorani were forced to relocate as the government relentlessly reduced the original twenty thousand square kilometers of Waorani territory to two thousand square kilometers in order to accommodate the oil interests.[266]

And contrary to the claims of many anthropologists, the missionaries *did* respect Waorani culture as much as they could, including the Waorani's hunting skills and their unique knowledge of the rainforest. The missionaries were not there to destroy culture but to introduce the unevangelized to the One who had created them for relationship with Himself. Admittedly the missionaries made decisions which, although intended to be in the best interests of the Waorani, did not always prove to be so.[267] Yet:

> In spite of possible mixed motives, the Saint family spent years living among the Huaorani, and handed them back their autonomy by training them to provide medical care and dental care for themselves. They also trained Huaorani (ironically including the son of the original troublemaker who got the five missionaries killed) to fly specialized aircraft which permit them to run their intertribal government, and to assist in getting injured villagers to their own Huaorani run clinic. The international interest in exploiting oil from Huaorani tribal lands does not take away the fact that, thanks to these missionaries, the Huaorani entered the 21st century

with some ability to deal with the outside world and confront their exploiters, who were already on the way . . . .[268]

And, by the way, *Time Magazine's* list of the most influential people of 2020 included a Waorani leader, Nemonte Nenquimo (Neh-mōn'-tā' Nen'-kē'-mō). She along with other Waorani *did confront their exploiters* and won a lawsuit preventing oil developers from further encroaching on their land![269] Yes, THERE'S ALWAYS MORE TO EVERY STORY.

Snake Poison

Although when Jurgen Hergert, the "King of Snakes," recently emerged physically unscathed after spending one hundred days in a tiny room accompanied by twenty-four free roaming poisonous snakes, he frankly admitted that his experience had been one he would likely never choose to go through again. Actually, just the thought of such an ordeal is enough to make most of us cringe in horror!

Throughout human history serpents have regularly been objects of dread. Granted, to a large degree they have been victims of bad press, and naturalists who specialize in the study of reptiles–herpetologists–have explained away much of the mystery of serpent lore. Nevertheless, the fear which snakes inspire in so many of us remains. But so too does a strange fascination with the taming and handling of snakes–not to mention living in a room full of them![270]

And in order to really understand these phenomena, we must look beyond sharp fangs, poison glands, twisting coils, and subtle ways. The third chapter of *Genesis* records that Satan operated through the agency of a serpent in leading mankind into the terrors of sin and death, of a broken relationship with God. And it was upon the serpent that God first pronounced a curse. Ever since, serpents have been associated with evil and the consequences which sinners suffer. (Genesis 3)

Jesus characterized the religious leaders who opposed Him as "serpents," the "brood of vipers" (Matthew 23:33 ESV). Isaiah described the evil deeds of his generation as the offspring of "adders' eggs" (Isaiah 59:5 ESV). Jeremiah portrayed the forces with which Babylon would bring God's judgment upon Judah as "adders for which there is no charm" (Jeremiah 8:17 ESV). Then, of course, there were the literal "fiery serpents" through which God chastised His complaining people during their wilderness wanderings (Numbers 21:6 NKJV). Serpents, in fact, symbolize a whole host of hostile forces which man finds arrayed against him, forces he constantly struggles to overcome. Thus, the fear and the fascination.

Yet although, as James says, man has managed to tame all kinds of serpents (James 3:7 KJV), he is unable to achieve mastery over the most deadly serpents of all: Satan and sin. The *Bible* makes it clear, beginning as early as the very same chapter of Genesis in which Satan and sin first raised their ugly heads (Genesis 3), that these archenemies of human souls would eventually be overcome. Though the serpent would "strike" the heel of the woman's seed, her seed would "crush" his head. (Genesis 3:15 NIV)

And such actions as God providing Adam and Eve with coats of skin to cover their nakedness, and animal sacrifices to inform them that "without the shedding of blood" there could be no forgiveness of sin (Hebrews 9:22 NASB), foreshadowed the fact that *He Himself* would be the One Who would come to man's rescue: "For God so loved the world that He gave His one and only Son" (John 3:16 NIV)–the "Lamb of God Who takes away the sin of the world" (John 3:16 NKJV).

Certainly, a lamb, representing innocence and righteousness, and a serpent, representing guilt and iniquity, present a striking contrast. Yet, in order that we might be delivered from Satan's power, in order that we night be forgiven and God's justice still be satisfied, in order that we might be freed from the power of sin, it was the sinless Lamb of God Who had to die. However, during those final hours before the Lord Jesus gave up His Spirit in death, a most astonishing transformation took place.

In becoming our substitute, in taking our guilt upon Himself, the innocent Lamb "was made to be sin": in the eyes of the Father, He became guilty of all our sins, the perpetrator of all of man's acts of rebellion. He became an accursed thing in order that there would one day be no more curse (Galatians 3:16; Revelation 22:3). For you see, it was not as the guiltless Lamb that our Savior was forsaken by His Father, but as the embodiment of all our sin—as a serpent.

You see, as the Israelites wandered in the wilderness and complained against God and Moses, God sent poisonous snakes among them, and many of the people were bitten and died. However, when the rest acknowledged their sin, God had Moses prepare a bronze serpent and place it on a pole. From then on, whoever was bitten and looked at the bronze snake would live. (Numbers 24:4-9)

Subsequently, "As Moses lifted up the serpent in the wilderness, even so must the Son of Man be lifted up" so that all who believe will have eternal life (John 3:14-16 KJV). Yes, THERE'S ALWAYS MORE TO EVERY STORY.

Spycraft

✦ ✦ ✦ ✦ ✦ ✦

The importance of a country's intelligence gathering capabilities to its national security can hardly be overemphasized. Spies are definitely essential government-funded personnel! And in spite of speculation over the relative effectiveness of the American CIA and the Soviet KGB, a significant number of military analysts consider Israeli intelligence to be the best in the world. The record of Israel's success in warfare with Egypt, Jordan, Lebanon, and especially Syria, certainly appears to support such a conclusion.[271]

But then, the Israelis have a long history of successful spy activity. Remember the conquest of Jericho? Joshua, the Israeli leader, had sent spies to check out the lay of the land and infiltrate the city. However, their cover was blown sometime after they entered Jericho. As their enemies closed in, it was only Rahab's quick action which saved them (Joshua 2). And centuries later, one of Rahab's descendants would be born in Bethlehem and hailed as the Savior of all who place their trust in Him!

Concern for their own safety and for their need to gain access to useful information has led spies to use a variety of ingenious techniques. They have assumed false identities, become masters of disguise and impersonation, and used forged documents in order to gain access to enemy secrets and avoid discovery. Some spies spend years patiently working their way into positions of trust and responsibility in order to operate above suspicion in the very nerve centers of enemy activity–to become what in spy jargon are known as "moles."

Typically, persons whose native tongue is not English are betrayed by their accent. So, for example, if Russian spies are to pass as Americans, they must eliminate their tell-tale pronunciation. And in addition, they must immerse themselves in the study of American culture. Once in America they have no trouble fooling their neighbors and gradually developing relationships which could ultimately provide access to vital information. Even then, however, they may eventually be found out, as was the case in a recent FBI probe.[272]

Perhaps *most* effective are those spies who choose to betray their own countries: they do not leave an initial trail of deceit and may have gained access to top-secret information even before their betrayal. One of the most audacious instances of such betrayal involved five British college students recruited by the Russian KGB while attending Cambridge University. Eventually known as "The Cambridge Five," this spy ring "passed information to the Soviet Union during World War II and was active from the 1930s until at least into the early 1950s."[273] And although these home-grown spies were ultimately unmasked, they were never prosecuted, apparently to avoid embarrassment to British security agencies![274] But none of the techniques devised by spies to enhance their safety and provide access to vital information can compare with the technique employed by Israel's super spy.

Once spies have obtained desirable information, they are still faced with the ticklish problem of getting it into the proper hands. In some cases they may be able to pass it on in the innocent guise of, say, a letter to a friend. Encrypted in a secret code, hidden in a micro-dot, rendered innocuous or invisible, it passes under the very eyes of the censor. In other cases the information may be borne by carrier pigeon, hidden in a secret compartment, deposited in a prearranged "mailbox", or transferred to an accomplice at a secret rendezvous or even in plain sight!

But regardless of the elaborate precautions they take and the creative methods they employ, every spy "lives a life of danger."[275] One slip, one miscalculation, one unguarded moment, and all may be lost. For this reason—and thanks to the technology now available—more and more emphasis is being placed on the development of *remote* surveillance techniques: the ability to spy—to collect intelligence data—from a distance. Electronic listening devices, reconnaissance aircraft, and spy satellites offer greater security to a spy network and longer life to a spy. And it is Israel 's super spy who must be credited with operating the most successful and foolproof remote intelligence gathering system ever devised.

Few people realize the extent of the role played by Israeli intelligence in the conflict with Syria. Israel's super spy was able to regularly access top secret Syrian military planning sessions, enabling Israeli commanders to develop incredibly successful counterstrategies. In fact, so completely did the Israelis anticipate enemy movements that the Syrian Commander in Chief ultimately became convinced there was a traitor in his very midst.

But then he learned that even the words spoken in his bedroom were immediately accessed at a distant spy listening-post located in Israel—in the town of Dothan—by Israel's super spy. And none of the high-tech devices which assist spies in gathering intelligence today had even been developed! Nevertheless, Elisha the prophet—Israel's super spy—was able to access intelligence gathered remotely by the most effective means possible: the omniscience of the ever-present God of Israel. (II Kings 6:8-23) Yes, THERE'S ALWAYS MORE TO EVERY STORY.

Step of Faith

<hr />

The phrase "walk a tightrope" suggests that a situation requires proceeding with extreme precision and caution in order to avoid an unwanted result. In extreme cases, the situation is a matter of life or death.[276] Dating back at least to ancient Greece and Rome, tightrope walking was a popular form of entertainment. Although it involved a highly tuned sense of balance and extraordinary acrobatic skill, it was never considered a sport and never included in the Olympic Games. Nevertheless, the remarkable abilities and focused commitment of the tightrope walker are awe inspiring.[277]

As tightrope walking developed, various flourishes were added to performances. While on the tightrope, funambulists (rope walkers) did summersaults and other gymnastic stunts, pushed wheelbarrows and rode bicycles, walked with stilts, walked backwards, had their wrists and ankles chained, and even performed with blindfolds on. Funambulists would also work together, two or more mounting a tightrope and choreographing their walks. One funambulist is even alleged to have ridden a horse up a wire to a high tower and back again![278]

In earlier times, tightrope walking was often associated with magic and occult powers. Tightrope walkers were featured at important public events, from coronations to royal marriages. If the performers survived their daring routines, it was taken as a good omen for those being honored.[279]

In 1859, Frenchman Jean-François Gravelet, known professionally as Blondin, became the first person to cross the gorge below Niagara Falls on a tightrope. As is true of most funambulists, he planned and practiced tirelessly in order to prepare for his performances. Even so, many considered him mad. Yet he crossed over successfully to the amazement of thousands of onlookers.[280]

Before one of his later crossings, he asked those gathered whether they believed he could take someone across with him. They enthusiastically indicated that they did. But when Blondin asked for a volunteer, their enthusiasm evaporated. Blondin's quest for a volunteer to join him on the tightrope reminds us that "faith without works is dead," that genuine biblical faith enables us to act when God calls. In this case, Blondin's manager showed enough faith in his friend that he volunteered to go, and the next day Blondin carried him on his back across the Canyon.[281]

In one variation Blondin carried along a portable stove, cooked an omelet halfway across, and lowered it to the Maid of the Mist sightseeing boat where those who tasted it gave it five stars![282] Meanwhile, other funambulists came up with their own versions of the crossing. But following a crossing in 1896, no further attempts were made for the next 115 years.[283]

But in 2012, Nik Wallenda, one of a long line of Wallenda aerialists dating back to the 1700s in Europe, became the first person to cross directly over any of the three falls that make up Niagara—in this case the Canadian Horseshoe Falls, the widest.[284]

His Niagara Falls crossing, and other world record or notable wire feats, further pushed the tightrope walking envelope. These spectacular achievements included participating in the first eight-person aerial pyramid, making the longest and highest bicycle crossings, being first to cross a tributary gorge of the Grand Canyon, making the steepest ascent of an inclined rope, completing the highest walk made wearing a blindfold, and walking over a live volcano in Nicaragua.[285]

The daring routines of funambulists have caused some to conclude that wire walkers are driven by a death wish. Yet Nik Wallenda is married, is the father of three, and plans to be around long enough to know his great grandchildren. And perhaps some of his descendants will continue the tradition of the Flying Wallendas.[286]

As for Nik, he believes that he has been gifted in a special way, and given a unique platform from which to bring glory to God.[287] Nik's crossings have had perilous moments, but he believes he is never alone:

> Wallenda credits God for his success, saying that what he does on the high-wire is a gift from God. He grew up in "a *Bible*-believing, God-fearing family" and describes himself as a "born-again Christian." Faith is "the most important part of my life," Nik says. Before every wire walk, Wallenda joins his family in prayer, and he always wears a cross as he performs. He remarks, "The Bible says pray without ceasing and I'm always praying." He denies that his stunts "test" God. "To test God would be to never train, never practice, and then to walk across the Grand Canyon; or to jump off a building, or throw myself in front of a truck."[288]

Yes, Nik Wallenda's astounding accomplishments have given him a unique opportunity to bear witness to the greatest accomplishment in human history–the forgiveness, justification, and sanctification of God's fallen image bearers through the work of Jesus. Yes, THERE'S ALWAYS MORE TO EVERY STORY.

Story Time

There's nothing quite like a good story. Many communicators ignore this fact, sometimes to their own disadvantage. Depending on exactly what they're attempting to communicate, and to what particular audience, stories can be extremely effective. If the primary objective is to communicate truth, one particularly well-respected communicator used stories extensively.

Yes, Jesus lived out and told stories to illustrate the nature of His Kingdom and the characteristics of His followers. He revealed what the lost lacked; told of the lost being found, born again, and taking up a cross; and pictured Himself as a vine and His followers as fruit-bearing branches. He told of the good Samaritan, the prodigal son, the faith of lepers and Gentiles, and is Himself the central character in the greatest story ever told.

The story tellers in ancient people groups were specially regarded as the repositories of a group's history and traditions. Their narratives were passed on orally to successive generations of story tellers. With the advent of written language, these histories and traditions could be meticulously copied down by hand and reach a wider audience. In this way, the books of the *Bible* were composed and assembled under Divine inspiration. And much of the completed *Scriptures* consist of narratives–stories–some historical, some symbolic.

Some of the parables Jesus told may have been historical, others symbolic, but their purpose in either case was always to convey Divine truth. Copying and translating the *Scriptures* were taken so seriously that few differences are to be found between the oldest available manuscripts and modern versions, none affecting essential Christian doctrines.[289] The development of moveable type and the printing press in Europe resulted in making the *Guttenberg Bible* and other translations available to a much broader audience. The possibility of a *Bible* in every home moved closer to reality.[290]

The ultimate effectiveness of biblical stories as one means God uses to change people's lives is of course reflected in the stories of those whose lives have been changed. Some of these stories appear in the *Bible* itself, such as the story of Nicodemus, a Pharisee and member of the Jewish ruling council who came to Jesus to inquire about the purpose of Jesus' ministry. In response, Jesus began to tell Nicodemus a story that did not begin with "Once upon a time" but with a far more puzzling statement: "I tell you the truth, unless you are born again, you cannot see the kingdom of God" (*John* 3:3 NLT)). When Nicodemus took this declaration literally, Jesus went on to share its real meaning. And in John 19:39 we find that Jesus' story had resulted in Nicodemus acknowledging Him as the Messiah.

On Christmas Eve 1906, Canadian born inventor Reginald Aubrey Fessenden broadcast what many believe to be the very first public radio program:

> He played O Holy Night on the violin and read a passage from Luke Chapter 2. . . . [A]nd the heavens did indeed declare the glory of God on that night. . . . His transmission proved that it was possible to fulfill the Great Commission (Matthew 28:19-20) . . . to bring the gospel to the ends of the earth.[291]

In 1922, Paul Rader, pastor of the Chicago Gospel Tabernacle, was invited by Chicago's mayor to expand Rader's rapidly growing ministry into the realm of radio. Broadcasting from the roof of city hall, Rader began what became a multi-faceted radio program featuring both preaching and music.

One of those saved while listening in person to Rader preach at a church in Los Angles was Charles Fuller, whose *Old Fashioned Revival Hour* was the first long-lived national broadcast of the Gospel.[292] "Aided by his wife, Grace, the Old Fashioned Revival Hour program created a family-like atmosphere."[293] Leading up to and during direct American participation in WWII it attracted an audience of over ten million listeners nationally and twenty million worldwide. "At its height during World War II, it surpassed in popularity virtually every show on American radio."[294]

No wonder then that Billy Graham's 1949 Los Angeles Crusade was brought to the attention of many through its promotion by Fuller, including the participation of Fuller and Grace in one of Graham's Crusade meetings.[295] Less than two weeks later, Fuller's association with Graham helped launch the young evangelist into "national prominence" when the media became aware that such well-known persons as Louis Zamperini (Olympian and war hero) had been converted at Graham's crusade.[296]

As Christian radio continued to develop, a number of stations began broadcasting programs which featured dramatizations of *Bible* stories, as well as stories of people—some real and some fictional—whose lives were changed by biblical narratives. *The Family Theater* and *The Greatest Story Ever Told* were examples.[297] Today there are other popular Christian radio dramas including those produced by Focus on the Family.[298]

But there is one particular Christian radio program that spans the decades from the Golden Age of Radio right up to the present, *and* exclusively dramatizes true stories about people who have been changed as they came to know Jesus. It's a program "that makes you face yourself and think" and tells of real people "whose lives and minds and hearts have been *Unshackled!*"[299]

Unshackled! is produced every week by Chicago's Pacific Garden Mission and is the longest continually-produced radio drama in history, "telling how God changes lives."[300] By the end of 2020, over thirty-six hundred different episodes had been produced and recorded live at the Mission over a span of seventy-plus years.[301] Today these stories are heard around the world in fifteen languages and are broadcast more than fifteen thousand times each week over the airwaves and internet.[302]

So why not take in a live recording session next time you're in Chicago![303] Yes, THERE'S ALWAYS MORE TO EVERY STORY!

The Call to Culture

When Adam and Eve were created and given stewardship over the earth, God told them that they and their descendants were to bear children, spread out over the earth, and utilize its resources in the process of developing culture (Genesis 1:26-28)—a big order since culture is the totality of the material, behavioral, intellectual, and moral characteristics of society![304]

And to motivate, guide, and equip us in the development of culture, God provided His personal presence and encouragement, and the requisite God-like abilities implicit in being created in His image. And even though our forebears rebelled against Him, we are still expected to fulfill His original commission, though under different circumstances.

What had originally been toil-less pleasure now requires us to work "in the sweat of [our] brow" in order to offset the opposing forces, both natural and of our own making, arrayed against us (Genesis 3:19 NIV). Fire, weather, floods, thorns, thistles, and infestations can destroy crops that farmers have taken great pains to grow. And human behaviors can reap devastation as well.

While we routinely attempt to devise and utilize means of minimizing the damage done by natural causes, we are far too often unwilling and unable to address our own reckless behavior and pursue reconciliation among ourselves. The solution to this second problem requires that we can at least agree on some mutually acceptable standard of behavior by which to proceed . . . and are willing to abide by it. And since our mutual cooperation is critical to culture-building, God has made it possible for us to work together in harmony if we apply His Word in the power of the Holy Spirit.

Thus, in the past, Christians have not only given witness to the truth, called people to repent, and helped them grow in grace and good works, but they have also made important cultural contributions in other ways. Some of the many cultural contributions of Christianity include the influence of Jesus' teachings on government, on the value of human life, and on the status of women; the architectural, engineering, artistic, and musical legacy of the great cathedrals; the preservation of knowledge and literacy, and the unification of Europe, which the church made possible following the fall of the Roman Empire; the promotion of learning in church schools and universities; and the church's encouragement of social services including health care and welfare.[305]

And although, as Christians, our permanent citizenship is in heaven, as long as we're also citizens of this present age we're still called upon to participate in the further development of culture. While it will not be until Christ returns that all will be made right, there is a process of "substantial healing" going on in the "here and now" as Christians speak to and actively develop culture along biblical lines. By word and example, Christians can be an influence for good—salt and light.[306]

The Apostle Paul indicates how and why we should seek the good of the land we are living in:

> I urge you, first of all, to pray for all people. Ask God to help them; intercede on their behalf, and give thanks for them. Pray this way for kings and all who are in authority so that we can live peaceful and quiet lives marked by godliness and dignity. This is good and pleases God our Savior, who wants everyone to be saved and to understand the truth. (I Timothy 2:1-4 NLT)

117

And as we seek to herald the Good News, we may find ourselves enhancing culture in biblically consistent ways. Consider the ministry of Martin Luther. Educated in classical and biblical learning from his youth, he entered law school at the age of twenty-two. But a few weeks later he was "besieged by the terror and agony of sudden death" in a powerful thunderstorm and vowed to enter a monastery if he survived.[307] True to his word, he became a Catholic priest and a Doctor of Theology.[308]

However, his study of *Scripture* led him to challenge the validity of certain Catholic teachings and practices. At the heart of his objections was the teaching that both *good works* and *God's gift of grace* are necessary for salvation. Of course, this, along with a number of other key objections to Catholic doctrine, eventually led to the divide between Catholicism and Protestantism known as the Reformation.[309]

But a lesser-known result of Luther's ministry followed in the wake of his translation of the *New Testament* into German. Luther believed that the *Bible* is the sole source and guide for Christian faith and practice, and that all people should be able to read it for themselves in order to verify the truth of the church's teaching. Consequently, he set out to translate the *New Testament* into a German dialect that could be understood by all Germans. Five hundred thousand copies of his translation were printed during his remaining years.[310]

Since his translation emphasized the meanings of *Bible* passages using familiar German phrases, figures of speech. and sentence structure, it was now much easier for even illiterate hearers to understand what the *Bible* revealed. Fascinatingly, Luther's ability to reach the masses by developing a unifying German language led to the Catholic Church printing its *own* version of the *Bible in the dialect Luther used.* In fact, Luther's adaptation of the German language helped *unify* Germany and *was the dialect used* in the ensuing theological debates between Luther and the Catholic church![311] Yes, THERE'S ALWAYS MORE TO EVERY STORY.

The Cure

———— ✦✦✦✦✦ ————

"In this world nothing can be certain but death and taxes," or so goes the old saying. And while taxes are inevitably raised, it would seem that many believe the dead are not. Although Adam and Eve initially had access to the tree of life, they were expelled from the Garden, and no one on earth has had access since (Genesis 3:22-24). Ever since then humans have been confronted with the inevitability of death.

Advances in biological and medical science have made it possible to extend the lives of individuals, but there is no cure for death. Some, such as psychologist Sigmund Freud, challenge us to dispense with wishful thinking and resign ourselves to the fact that the universe is unforgiving, and death terminates our existence.[312]

This seems to be the attitude of rock climber Alex Honnold, who in 2017 became the first person to *free solo* (climb without ropes) nearly 3000 feet to the top of El Capitan in Yosemite National Park. Honnold "describes himself as a militant, anti-religion atheist."[313] He, like other atheists who engage in death-defying extreme sports to give meaning to their brief existence, obviously believes that "Nature doesn't care" whether he lives or dies. But while most atheists who engage in extreme sports are primarily seeking thrills as well as accomplishment, the part of Honnold's brain that governs emotional responses has been shown to be "barely" activated in fear-inducing situations. Thus, rather than seeking thrills during his ascents, he is able to focus more fully on his next move.[314] It would seem that while climbing, only a final fall into oblivion could divert his concentration.

But although "Nature" may not care, people *do* value other people–and even animals–who care about them. And throughout history, most people have sought to extend their lives rather than end them prematurely. At the least, wherever possible they have taken reasonable precautions to avoid or overcome life threatening situations. And both Freud and Honnold did so.

Methods and substances that can extend life have been sought from well before the time of Ponce de León and the elusive fountain of youth.[315] In ancient Egypt, mummification was intended to keep a dead body preserved so that the spirit within it would not be lost and thereby prevented entrance into the afterlife.[316] In modern times, some have arranged to be cryogenically frozen when they die, in hopes that advances in technology will allow them to be reanimated. The most famous of these is baseball legend Ted Williams.[317] Meanwhile, scientists hope to someday be able to transfer all of a person's memories from their brain to a permanent storage medium, at least keeping their *thoughts* alive indefinitely.[318]

Throughout time, most people have sought comfort in the belief that when death does occur, it's not the end. Such theistic or transcendent beliefs come in a number of irreconcilable flavors including monism, polytheism, monotheism, and spiritism.

Spiritists believe that when a person dies, their spirit lives on, and that departed spirits can communicate with and influence the lives of humans. Many "isms" also teach that spirits continue to evolve through successive reincarnations during which they grow in wisdom and compassion. Some point to Jesus as having reached the highest level of spiritual development.

People involved in spiritism are often portrayed seeking to make contact with departed loves ones. Well-known individuals who attempted to do so include Mary Todd Lincoln (Abraham Lincoln's wife), and Arthur Conan Doyle (creator of Sherlock Holmes).[319]

In addition, near-death experiences are offered as convincing evidence of an afterlife. Meanwhile, tales of people being raised from the dead–though eventually dying–persist. Yes, it would definitely seem a good idea to spend at least as much time *researching* the possibility of eternal life and how to attain it as extreme sports experts and others in dangerous undertakings spend *planning* in order to *avoid* death!

One person who set out to disprove the resurrection of Jesus was an award-winning reporter for the *Chicago Tribune* and other newspapers. As he meticulously researched the matter, he was eventually forced to acknowledge the overwhelming weight of evidence for the return of Jesus from the dead.

Yet intellectual assent is not the same as a personal relationship with the Creator. Jesus said, "No one can come to me, unless the Father who sent me makes them want to come. But if they do come, I will raise them to life on the last day" (John 6:44 CEV). And Lee Strobel wanted to come. Today he is no longer a secular reporter but a herald of the Good News: that God offers us eternal life through His amazing grace, as Strobel documented in his book *The Case for Christ*.[320] And yes, THERE'S ALWAYS MORE TO EVERY STORY.

The Ethiopian Eunuch

The person referred to in our story's title was one of those Gentile believers whose names are scattered throughout the pages of *Scripture* and whose faith shines brightly amidst a period of national Jewish decline. As God's covenant people, the Jews experienced success or failure on the national scene depending on their corporate obedience to the terms of the covenant. From the time of the exodus onward, the nation passed through countless cycles of rebellion, retribution, repentance, and restoration.[321]

A corrupt leadership and a general spiritual blindness in His day caused Jesus to note that:

> there were many widows in Israel in Elijah's time, when the sky was shut for three and a half years and there was a severe famine throughout the land. Yet Elijah was not sent to any of them, but to a widow in Zarephath in the region of Sidon. And there were many in Israel with leprosy in the time of Elisha the prophet, yet not one of them was cleansed—only Naaman the Syrian." (Luke 4:25-27 NIV).

Among those Jesus encountered in His own ministry were the Syrophoenician woman from whose daughter He cast a demon, and whom He commended saying, "O woman, great is your faith" (Matthew 15:28 ESV); and the Roman centurion whose servant He healed and at whom He "marveled," announcing, "I have not found such great faith even in Israel" (Luke 7:9 ESV).

And following the Lord's ascension, those who spread the good news would turn increasingly to the Gentiles . . . "in Jerusalem and in all Judea, and Samaria, and as far as the remotest part of the earth" (Acts 1:8 NASB). Philip and Peter were among the first of Jesus' followers to discover Gentile hunger for the Savior, and Paul considered himself "an apostle to the Gentiles" (Romans 11:13 NKJV).

Yes, the Ethiopian eunuch referred to at the beginning of our story belongs to an illustrious company of Biblical heroes who were Gentiles. It isn't necessary to even identify him by name because he is principally known by his nationality and his role as a servant to royalty. The precise details of his introduction to the God of Israel are unknown, but certainly from the time of Israel's deliverance from Egypt and the nation's defeat of hostile forces both within and surrounding the Land of Promise, word of God's might and blessings spread far and wide.

Moreover, as the nation conducted ever increasing trade and capital growth during its Golden Age, foreign potentates such as the Queen of Sheba could not help but be impressed by what Israel's God had done for the nation (I Kings 10:7). And later, when Jews were forcibly removed from their homeland and taken to Assyria and Babylon, further opportunities for the Word of the LORD to take root in Gentile soil were provided. As to the Ethiopian eunuch, it is clear that this Gentile servant of royalty had been introduced to the *Scriptures*, found them relevant to Gentiles as well as Jews, and accepted them as the very Word of God.

Thus the God whom all but a remnant of His chosen people had rejected was honored in His own chosen way and place by a foreigner. And God in turn honored the eunuch by revealing His will to him through one of His special spokesmen. As he had pondered the words of one of the prophets, this servant of royalty had become extremely perplexed. And he could hardly have known without additional instruction that some of the prophet's words referred to the coming Messiah.

This was the very same prophet through whom the LORD had said, "Can the Ethiopian change his skin or the leopard his spots?" to indicate how set in their evil ways the majority of the Jews of that day were (Jeremiah 13:23 ESV). Words conveying a similar meaning were used to bring God's message of salvation to the anxious ears of an Ethiopian servant of royalty–a eunuch.

While most of the Jews had rejected what the prophet Jeremiah had proclaimed about the salvation and judgment of God, including the imminent destruction of Jerusalem, this Ethiopian clung faithfully to what he knew of God's Word. And he took his life in his hands in doing so. For you see, this Ethiopian eunuch was the servant of King Zedekiah of Judah, last in the line of Israeli kings prior to the destruction of Jerusalem by Babylon. It was this Gentile servant who rescued Jeremiah after some Jewish princes had thrown him into a pit and left him to die because his predictions were disheartening the army and the general population. (Jeremiah 38)

Soon after his rescue, Jeremiah was directed by the LORD to inform Ebed-Melech, the Ethiopian eunuch, that although disaster was in store for Jerusalem, neither the princes who sought his life for rescuing Jeremiah, nor the invading Babylonians, would harm him. (Jeremiah 39):

> 'For I will certainly rescue you, and you will not fall by the sword; but you will have your *own* life as booty, because you have trusted in Me,' declares the Lord. (Jeremiah 39:18 NASB 1995).

Thus a Gentile, an Ethiopian eunuch, saved the life of a prophet who wrote of the demise of the nation of Israel, its future restoration, and its coming Messiah. And it would be over four hundred years later that *another* Ethiopian eunuch would be reading the book of Jeremiah's predecessor Isaiah, and with the help of an evangelist named Philip, learn that the Messiah had come at last! (Acts 8:26-39) Yes, THERE'S ALWAYS MORE TO EVERY STORY.

The Evil Empire

On March 8, 1983, President Ronald Reagan spoke to the National Association of Evangelicals, characterizing the Soviet Union as an "evil empire."[322] Leading up to the Cold War, Soviet Russia had become a nation whose sphere of influence had spread as her military might grew. And there were nations both near and far which had provoked Soviet antagonism but had not yet fallen victim to Russia's brutal quest for world domination. Yet, these nations lived in constant dread, the threat of subjugation or annihilation hanging like the sword of Damocles over their collective heads.

Year after year, Russia's leaders had zealously devoted their energies to the achievement of military superiority—to counteract fear of enemy invasion, and to advance their program of conquest. And eventually, Russia became perhaps the most formidable of military powers.

Since the Russian Revolution in the first quarter of the twentieth century, those who attempted to oppose the new regime were put down in cruel and relentless fashion. The country's official rejection of the God of the *Bible* left it free to employ any and every means to achieve its ultimate purpose. Indeed, the communist government took the lives of countless opponents, and enslaved and otherwise ill-treated multitudes more. It seemed fitting that Russia was symbolized by a savage beast of prey—a bear! And those people Soviet Russia brought under its power were pressured, propagandized, and brainwashed to coerce them into adopting its evil ways.

Along with Russia's growing power came an increasing arrogance and sense of near invincibility. Parades held in Red Square, the vast plaza fronting the strongly fortified complex known as the Kremlin, the seat of national government, showcased Russia's crack troops and vast array of military hardware. The totalitarian leadership constantly stirred up both pride in the country's military might and fear of her enemies, keeping the masses convinced that military superiority must come first, regardless of the sacrifices in comfort which had to be endured. For Russia was locked in an arms race with forces determined to curb her political ambitions and, if necessary, to negate her power totally.

Yet even as this nation pursued its relentless course, an event took place which, under the circumstances, seemed highly improbable. In 1982, and again in 1984, evangelist Billy Graham, a citizen of one of Russia's most outspoken adversaries and a representative of a religion to which the Soviet government was officially and, not uncommonly, violently opposed, was allowed to make an unprecedented journey across the sea to the nation's heartland. There he was not only permitted to speak in public, but to do so *without censorship*.[323] He used the opportunity to call on the people of Russia to repent of their sins and experience peace with God. And there was a tremendous response to his message.[324]

But regrettably, the nation as a whole has failed to turn from its bent toward military conquest. Although the Soviet Union was somewhat dismantled when the Russian Federation was formed in 1991 and the Cold War supposedly ended, there are even now signs of continuing hostility toward other countries, including Israel and the United States.

Yet the prophetic words of Ezekiel and others in *Scripture* have been taken by some *Bible* expositors to indicate that this nation, powerful as she may be, is doomed to destruction. Even as Billy Graham spoke, the nation was shaping plans to deal with strategic problems associated with the existence of Israel. These plans have not yet resulted in war with Israel, but there have been times in Israel's history when other "evil empires" *did* invade Israel.[325]

For example, several empires with ambitions similar to those which Russia has pursued have successfully invaded Israel. The first was destroyed over twenty-four hundred years ago—so completely that until recently its very existence had been in doubt. But now, archeological discoveries have confirmed the Biblical account, establishing this mighty nation's place in history. That nation, so irreverent and ruthless, so powerful and determined, was Assyria.[326] The showplace of its military might and idolatrous practices was Nineveh. And, of course, the evangelist whose remarkable journey landed him in enemy territory was Jonah.

And as occurred in Russia when Billy Graham reminded his hearers of the consequences of sin, people "turned from their evil ways" (Jonah 3:10 NIV). For the Ninevites, there was a reprieve from God's judgment. However, one of the prophets for whom a book of the *Bible* was named predicted that the reprieve which God gave to the Ninevites would be short-lived, and that the Assyrian Empire would be destroyed after its conquest of Israel's northern kingdom. In this instance God used the Babylonian military to carry out His judgment. And the resulting destruction was so complete that it was not until the 1840s that the full extent of the Assyrian Empire and the fabled grandeur of the city of Nineveh were authenticated.

And who was the prophet who had foretold this empire's ultimate doom? He was one of the twelve *minor* prophets, but minor only in the sense that their namesake books are shorter than some of the Bible's other prophetic books. If you haven't done so before, you might want to check out what Nahum had to say![327] Yes, THERE'S ALWAYS MORE TO EVERY STORY.

The King of Counterpoint

The pipe organ was invented by the Greek engineer Ctesibius (Teh-sib´-ē-us) of Alexandria sometime during the third century B.C.[328] But it was not until approximately thirteen hundred years later that it began to be integrated into the life of the church.[329] Pipe organs are the largest musical instruments. And the largest pipe organ, determined by the number of pipes it contains and other criteria, is the Boardwalk Hall Auditorium Organ in Atlantic City, New Jersey. It weighs about one hundred fifty tons and contains 33,114 pipes, the tallest and lowest in pitch being sixty-four feet long. The largest organ in a church setting is the Cadet Chapel Organ at the US Military Academy at West Point.[330]

One of the reasons the organ has become so common in churches is that it provides a range of notes which varies extensively both below and above the range of the human voice. As Pope Benedict XVI put it:

> In the Constitution on Sacred Liturgy of the Second Vatican Council (Sacrosanctum Concilium), it is emphasized that the "combination of sacred music and words ... forms a necessary or integral part of the solemn liturgy." . . . This means that music and song are more than an embellishment (perhaps even unnecessary) of worship; they are themselves part of the liturgical action. Solemn sacred music,

with choir, organ, orchestra and the singing of the people, is not therefore a kind of addition that frames the liturgy and makes it more pleasing, but an important means of active participation in worship. The organ has always been considered, and rightly so, the king of musical instruments, because it takes up all the sounds of creation . . . and gives resonance to the fullness of human sentiments, from joy to sadness, from praise to lamentation. By transcending the merely human sphere, as all music of quality does, it evokes the divine. The organ's great range of timbre, from piano through to a thundering fortissimo, makes it an instrument superior to all others. It is capable of echoing and expressing all the experiences of human life. The manifold possibilities of the organ in some way remind us of the immensity and the magnificence of God."[331]

John was the son of a seventh-generation musician who played the trumpet and violin and led his town's instrumental ensemble. The son showed a musical aptitude himself, learning to play the violin and developing a fine singing voice. At the age of fifteen, based on his vocal ability, he won a scholarship to a noted music school. There, however, he was more interested in further improving another skill he had begun developing–playing the organ. And he became so adept at playing this instrument that his talent eventually earned him employment at a number of locations where he would play the local church organ and conduct the musical education of the local youth.[332] He also became an expert in the art of organ construction, supervising the building and restoration of organs and testing their qualities.[333]

John persistently tried to make the best use of his time. Alas, wishing to move on from one of his positions to another which he considered more challenging, he was involved in a contract dispute with his employer and ended up in jail for most of a month. During this hiatus he began a year-long cycle of organ chorale preludes[334] and may have begun "The Well-Tempered Clavier," music which John composed for keyboard instruments. When the contract matter was settled, he moved on to his longest lasting and most productive period.[335]

During his lifetime, John was primarily known for his organ-playing virtuosity and teaching skills. Although some master musicians recognized his prowess as a composer, the techniques he developed or improved on in his particular genre of music were not widely appreciated by the general music public. He was *not* a celebrated composer in his own day. After his death at age sixty-five, his compositions were occasionally performed locally, but were otherwise of interest only to other professional musicians and to middle-class intellectuals who had a particular interest in the music of deceased composers.[336]

But this interest gradually spread to the broader population of music lovers. By the time one of the great musicians of the next generation, Felix Mendelssohn, arranged for John's–Johann Sebastian Bach's–*St. Matthew Passion* to be performed in a concert venue, contemporary musical enthusiasts, instead of focusing their interest solely on new musical works, were now ready to reexamine the qualities of compositions whose authors had died. And in Bach's case they judged those qualities to be *extraordinary*. Many now consider him the greatest composer ever.[337] Ludwig van Beethoven, born twenty years after Bach,

> called Bach the "Original father of harmony" and, in a pun on the literal meaning of Bach's name, "brook," Beethoven declared that Bach's music was so outstanding that his name should have been Meer, meaning "sea" ("not a brook, but a sea").[338]

Bach finally received the recognition he deserved for his contributions to what is known as the Baroque musical repertoire, and for his refinement of compositional techniques. Perhaps the technique he is best known for is the art of counterpoint: "the simultaneous sounding of separate melodies or lines 'against' each other."[339] Bach's most elaborate *contrapuntal* form was the fugue, which he raised to new heights.[340] Among his most famous works besides the *St. Matthew Passion* are the *Brandenburg Concertos, Goldberg Variations, Tocatta and Fugue in D Minor, Well-Tempered Clavier,* and *Jesu, Joy of Man's Desiring.*[341]

Above all, Bach felt that his musical work was a Divine calling. According to Michael Marissen of *The New York Times*:

> [He] understood himself less as a modern artist than as a preacher who was following his religious vocation.[342]

Bach believed the orthodox Lutheran position regarding sacred music:

> At a rendering of devout music, the "Grace-Presence" of God will always inhabit the hearts of Christian believers, whose bodies, according to the New Testament, are "a temple of the Holy Spirit."[343]

Accordingly, Bach always sought to elevate the words of his choral works above his musical settings, the musical accompaniment properly reinforcing the transcendent meaning and emotional power of the text. Bach never forgot that it was God who made the music through him. Whenever he began a new piece, he bowed his head and prayed, "Jesus, help me show your glory through the music I write. May it bring you joy even as it brings joy to your people." The letters JJ at the beginning of his compositions stood for *Jesu juva,*

Latin for "Jesus, help," and the letters SDG at the end for *soli Deo gloria*—"for God's glory alone."[344]

How ironic, in light of its important place in the life of the church, that one of the original uses of the pipe organ was to ramp up the fervor of the crowds in Greek and Roman arenas. Thus it was initially associated with gladiatorial fights and other deadly entertainments rather than the path to eternal life![345] Yes, THERE'S ALWAYS MORE TO EVERY STORY.

The Lion King

The male lion, with its shaggy mane and MGM roar, has so activated our imaginations that he has earned the title "King of Beasts." In their natural habitat, lions are stealthy predators, hardly to be mistaken for the cowardly lion in *The Wizard of Oz*! Some are indeed manhunters. Today, lions are found in the wild only in limited parts of central and southern Africa, but their past distribution included much more of Africa plus lands from Greece eastward all the way to India–including the land of Israel.[346] No wonder that as the Israelites prepared to conquer the land of promise, Moses informed them that "[l]ittle by little [the LORD] will drive out these nations as you advance. You will not be able to destroy them all at once, for, if you did, the number of wild animals would increase and be a threat to you" (Deuteronomy 7:22 GNT).

And the *Old Testament* documents a number of lion attacks, including one involving Samson, and another, the future king David. In fact, the *Bible* mentions lions in many places, and whether they're referenced literally, as in the account of Daniel and the lions' den, or figuratively, as when individuals who seek material possessions are referred to as "young lions," the emphasis is on strength, ferocity, and determination.[347]

In the beginning, God commissioned His image bearers to "[r]ule over the fish in the sea and the birds in the sky and over every living creature that moves on the ground" (Genesis 1:28 NIV). As a result, "every kind of beast and bird, of reptile and creature of the sea, is tamed and has been tamed by mankind" (James 3:7 NKJ). Even lions and tigers and bears? Oh my!

Several of the best-known lion tamers have been women, and they didn't necessarily limit their circus acts to lions. In the 1960s, Yvonne Berman performed with lions, tigers, leopards, black panthers, a polar bear, and a Himalayan bear.[348] And probably the most famous lion tamer of all, Clyde Beatty, entered the ring with a menagerie of forty male and female lions and tigers, and also worked with different mixes of lions, tigers, leopards, pumas, hyenas, and bears. Beatty gave his last performance in 1965 and passed away of natural causes later that same year. Fittingly, a lion is featured on his gravesite plaque.[349] Yet, in spite of their amazing ability to modify animal behavior, lion tamers are at risk during their acts, and many have been scarred, severely injured, and some even killed as a result of animal attacks.[350]

Occasionally, however, we hear about lions that actually accept humans as lifelong friends. Remember the folktale about Androcles and the lion? Androcles was a slave who escaped from his Roman master and fled to the forest. There he encountered a lion whose paw needed first aid. Androcles attended to the injury and earned the lion's gratitude. However, both were taken captive and sent to the arena, where Androcles was to be offered to the lion. But rather than attack Androcles, the lion lavished affection on him, and both were awarded their freedom.[351]

Then of course, there are C.S. Lewis's *Chronicles of Narnia*, featuring the lion Aslan. "But is He a safe lion?" one of the children in the first book—*The Lion, the Witch, and the Wardrobe*—asks. Wise Mr. Beaver replies, "Who said anything about safe? 'Course he isn't safe. But he's good. He's the King, I tell you. . . . He's wild, you know. Not like a tame lion."[352] And Jesus is pictured in the *Bible* as the Lion of the Tribe of Judah: He is both to be embraced as welcoming King and feared as righteous Judge.[353]

Perhaps you have heard about the two young men who purchased a lion cub and raised him in London until, after more than a year, they felt it was best to have him introduced to his natural habitat in Kenya. A year later, after learning that the lion had become the head of his own pride of lions, they flew to Kenya, not even sure he'd remember them. But they were overjoyed when they were welcomed by him in the very manner that Androcles had been greeted. And by the way, this lion was named "Christian" in rebuke of all those who had cheered as lions attacked Christians in Roman arenas.[354] Yes, THERE'S ALWAYS MORE TO EVERY STORY.

The Man Who Moved the Earth

+ + + + + +

Well before the Age of Steam and fuel-powered machinery, manpower, animal power, gravity, sledges, levers, wheels, rollers, flowing water, and barges were used in various combinations to make possible massive building projects that boggle the mind. Africa has the Great Pyramid of Giza, Europe has the Coliseum, and Asia has the Great Wall.

The oldest of these is the Great Pyramid, completed around 2550 B.C. It's composed of over two million primarily limestone blocks averaging two to two and a half tons apiece, with inner chambers containing granite blocks weighing up to eighty tons. Exactly how Egyptian engineers managed to have those blocks cut in distant quarries so they fit together precisely in the completed structure, then moved them to the construction site, remains a mystery.[355]

But the latest research suggests that Egyptian copper, and iron obtained from other countries, were fashioned into implements used to split the rock, and the finished blocks then levered out of the quarries using ropes, ramps, and brute strength.[356] Stone blocks from quarries near the Nile were barged in, while those quarried out in the desert were thought to have been loaded onto sledges which were then pulled with ropes across the sand while laborers sprinkled just enough water in front of the sledges to make the sand slippery. It is conjectured that by this means the force required to move them was cut in half.[357]

Ramps next to the growing pyramid were then likely used to move the blocks into place. When completed, at a height of 481 feet, it was the tallest structure yet built, and remained so for 3800 years![358]

The advent of steamships, railroads, suspension bridges, and skyscrapers in the 1800s reflected the growing technologies linked directly to the development of the steam engine and subsequent sources of machine power. Although the principle of steam power was known from the first century A.D., it was not until 1698 that the pressure cooker inspired Thomas Savery to invent the first true steam-powered machine, a machine which removed water from flooded mines. And the blast furnaces that separated iron, copper, and lead from the ores produced by the mines were soon greatly improved when steam power was used to produce the more powerful blasts of air needed to increase their efficiency.[359]

But it wasn't until the 1800s that the steam engine became the dominant power source in industrialized nations, including Britain and the US.[360] Up until then, running water was the primary source of machine power during the Industrial Revolution. But steam engines made it unnecessary for industries to locate near rivers. And as steam engines became more compact, more efficient, more powerful, and when necessary, portable, they transformed the face of industry.[361]

Children are often fascinated by pictures and toy versions of steam shovels, dump trucks, and other pieces of heavy equipment. Some carry that early interest into a future vocation. Perhaps Gilmore did, because at the age of fourteen he quit school and launched into a series of jobs and independent learning experiences which acquainted him with a wide variety of skills, from ironworker to mechanic to electrician to welder to farm laborer to miner to carpenter's apprentice to engineer, all of which served his visionary work in the field of heavy equipment.[362]

He began working with heavy equipment at the age of thirty-two as a regrading contractor. A year later he established a small production facility which enabled him to build earthmoving equipment of his own design. Contracted to build a road, he would invent, then build in his own facility, pieces of equipment which would enable him to complete the job more quickly and effectively.[363]

Eventually he turned his focus from contract jobs using his growing stable of heavy equipment, to *producing* that equipment to sell to other contractors. From the age of thirty-five until he was seventy-seven, he was granted patents for earthmoving equipment, other types of heavy equipment, manufacturing processes, and machine tools. Among those inventions were "the bulldozer, scrapers of all sorts, dredgers, portable cranes, rollers, dump wagons, bridge spans, logging equipment, mobile sea platforms for oil exploration, the electric wheel and many others."[364]

In fact, during his lifetime, Gilmore's company manufactured more of the largest and most innovative pieces of earth-moving and heavy industrial equipment than any other manufacturer on the planet![365] And the "Le Tourneau L-2350, is currently the world's largest rubber-tyred, front-end wheel loader, and holds the Guinness World Record for Biggest Earth Mover."[366]

But even more significantly,

> [Gilmore, that is, Robert Gilmore (R. G.)] LeTourneau, is perhaps the most inspiring Christian inventor, businessman and entrepreneur the world has ever seen. A sixth grade dropout, LeTourneau went on to become the leading earth moving machinery manufacturer of his day with plants on 4 continents, more than 300 patents to his name and major contributions to road construction and heavy equipment that forever changed the world. Most importantly, his contribution to the advancement of the Gospel ranks him among the greatest of

Christian Businessmen of all time. Famous for living on 10% of his income and giving 90% to the spread of the Gospel, LeTourneau exemplified what a Christian businessman should be.[367]

And by the way, during WWII, LeTourneau supplied nearly 70% of the earthmoving and material-handling equipment used by the Allied forces, including inventions he came up with during the war years and rushed into production to better meet the demands of the conflict. His essential contributions helped significantly shorten and win the war![368] Yes, THERE'S ALWAYS MORE TO EVERY STORY.

The Missing Piece

＋＋◆◆◆◆＋＋

I Love a Mystery was the title of an old-time radio drama which appealed to our natural desire to see puzzles solved and scoundrels brought to justice. The conclusions of such mysteries usually found the pieces put together and the perpetrators put away–or dead.[369]

But too-often overlooked in such stories is what follows the solution. How do those who have suffered loss handle the post-traumatic stress they may well be experiencing? And how do those responsible for that loss deal with knowledge of the suffering they caused? Other questions could be asked as well, such as: What could be done to prevent similar crimes? Does the punishment fit the crime? What good could possibly come from any particular case of victimization?

There are, thankfully, individuals and groups actively addressing these questions. The book *Dead Man Walking* documents the true story of a Catholic nun, Sister Helen Prejean, who became a spiritual counselor to men who were eventually executed for their crimes.[370] And in seeking to prepare them for that final walk, she became their friend and confidant as well. Furthermore, she founded an organization to help crime victims deal with their losses and advocated the elimination of capital punishment.[371]

Then there are those who have committed crimes, yet end up ministering to the victimized and to other victimizers as well. Remember Chuck Colson? Sentenced for illegal activity as aide to President Nixon, Jesus encountered him in prison, and he emerged a changed man. Subsequently, he helped countless prisoners and their families through his Prison Fellowship ministry. Today his prison work serves as a model for the most successful means of converting places of incarceration into actual reform-atories! And in addition, he has touched multitudes through his speaking, his books—including *Born Again* and *How Now Shall We Live*—and through The Colson Center for Christian Worldview. The Colson Center also provides an online presence with *Breakpoint*, a website providing Christian perspectives on current cultural trends.[372]

Granted, what Colson did was wrong, but it didn't call for an extended time in prison . . . or worse, the death penalty. And it would seem that, given his post-prison behavior, his eventual reinstatement into society was a realistic expectation. And although Sister Prejean was able to develop a personal friendship with prisoners who had committed the most horrific of crimes, she was neither their victim nor a victim's family member or friend. But in other cases, forgiveness just seems too much to ask!

The heart of becoming a Christian is a *changed* heart. What we would not or could not do apart from our relationship with Jesus becomes possible. We begin to live out His image in the power of the Holy Spirit. When Stephen was being stoned for sharing the truth, he imaged his Savior:

> While they were stoning him, Stephen prayed, "Lord Jesus, receive my spirit." Then he fell on his knees and cried out, "Lord, do not hold this sin against them." (Acts 7:59-60 NIV).

The willingness of Jesus to forgive is the key element in the way Christians are to relate to others as we are being conformed to His image. When Jesus' disciples asked Him to teach them how to pray, the model prayer He taught them includes the request that God "forgive us our sins, as we have forgiven those who have sinned against us" (Matthew 6:12 ISV).

So, what do we do if those who sin against us *don't ask* for our forgiveness? If we are to follow Jesus' example, we must at the very least be prepared to forgive them if they should eventually ask us to do so, perhaps even to forgive them even if they don't if their offense is relatively inconsequential. Moreover, if the civil justice system appropriately penalizes them for committing crimes which have victimized us, we may find it easier to pursue reconciliation than if they had gotten off scot-free. And in any case, we must leave their earthly fate in God's hands:

> Beloved, never avenge yourselves, but leave the way open for God's wrath [and His judicial righteousness]; for it is written [in Scripture], "VENGEANCE IS MINE, I WILL REPAY," says the Lord. . . . Do not be overcome and conquered by evil, but overcome evil with good. (Romans 12:19 and 21 AMP)

But the willingness to forgive which flows from a changed heart is most sorely tested when those victimizers who commit the gravest of offenses are *never* penalized by the judicial system and appear to be flourishing in their freedom. Certainly, a person who survived Nazi prison camps would not be expected to forgive one of their abusers who had gone unpunished. Imagine then, the amplified trauma a survivor would be subjected to if they should encounter one of their tormentors, especially if he was headed their way! One Holocaust survivor who found herself in that very situation was Corrie ten Boom.

She had been speaking about forgiveness in a church in Germany. Afterwards, a man whom she recognized as one of her former concentration camp guards approached her. Although he did not remember her, he acknowledged guilt for his cruel actions, said that he had become a Christian, and asked her forgiveness. Corrie relates her reaction in her book *The Hiding Place*:

And I stood there – I whose sins had every day to be forgiven – and could not. . . . I wrestled with the most difficult thing I ever had to do. . . . The message that God forgives has a prior condition: that we forgive those who have injured us. And still I stood there with the coldness clutching my heart. But forgiveness is not an emotion – I knew that too. Forgiveness is an act of the will. . . . "Jesus, help me! I prayed silently." I can lift my hand, . . . you supply the feeling." And so, woodenly . . . I thrust my hand into the one stretched out to me. And as I did, an incredible thing took place. The current started in my shoulder, raced down my arm, sprang into our joined hands. And then the healing warmth seemed to flood my whole being, bringing tears to my eyes. "I forgive you, brother!" I cried. "With all my heart!" For a long moment we grasped each other's hands, the former guard and the former prisoner. I had never known the love of God so intensely as I did then.[373]

Yes, THERE'S ALWAYS MORE TO EVERY STORY.

The Misunderstanding

+ ✦✦✦✦ +

The voyage of the Beagle was to influence worldviews in unanticipated ways. Before it, although atheists had been attempting to rationalize their world-without-God position since the scientific revolution and even before, the argument from design offered by Christian scientists and philosophers held sway in the public eye. The universe was purposeful, planned and produced by an all-knowing omnipotent Creator. And human beings were its high point, created in their Creator's image.[374]

The HMS Beagle, a Royal Navy sloop which had been refitted for use as a survey vessel, departed Britain in 1831 to survey the coastlines of Tierra del Fuego and other parts of Patagonia at the southern tip of South America. Those participating in the expedition included Charles Darwin, recently graduated from college. When Darwin saw the condition of society in Tierra del Fuego, he concluded that:

> For him, [the natives] occupied a low position in the human hierarchical scale – they were "miserable, degraded savages". Darwin believed that the difference between the "savages" and civilized man was greater than that between a wild animal and a domesticated animal.[375]

Meanwhile, Darwin made observations along the way—most notably in the Galapagos Islands off the coast of Ecuador—which helped influence him to propose that species evolve by means of a process of natural selection. Perhaps best known of his discoveries was the variation within the population of finches in the islands. He hypothesized that all of these finches had descended from a common ancestor, but that over time, random modifications in their features had produced new varieties, each suited to survive in a different part of a gradually changing environment. Most notably, each variety of finch had a bill with a distinctive size and shape, enabling it to specialize in using a food source different than those used by the other varieties.[376]

When his best-known book, *On the Origin of Species by Means of Natural Selection; or, The Preservation of Favoured Races in the Struggle for Life,* was published in *1859,*[377] it was not only enthusiastically welcomed by atheists, but also by some Christians as well. In spite of earlier estimates by notable Christians that the earth was around 4000 years old, by the time of Darwin, many Christians had come to accept that the earth was much much older. And there were some staunch Christians, including Frederick Temple, a future Archbishop of Canterbury,[378] and the distinguished Harvard biologist Asa Gray, who saw in Darwinism a confirmation of a distinct process of development within creation.[379] Having examined Darwin's book, Gray concluded:

> Finally, we advise nobody to accept Darwin's or any other derivative theory as true. The time has not come for that, and perhaps never will. We also advise against a similar credulity on the other side, in a blind faith that species—that the manifold sorts and forms of existing animals and vegetables—"have no secondary cause." . . . But we are confident, that, if a derivative hypothesis ever is established, it will be so on a solid theistic ground.[380]

Anglican theologian Aubrey Moore rejoiced in that under "the guise of a foe," Darwin had done "the work of a friend," liberating Christianity from a false image of the deity in which God was only present in the world when performing miracles. This false view of God, known as Deism, holds that the universe was created by God in the distant past, but then left to develop *without* His intervention. Moore decided that Darwin's position did *not* require that God determine *every* outcome in evolution by a special supernatural act, and that in doing science we are enabled to "think God's thoughts after Him." Thus Moore considered science a valid way of acquiring true knowledge. Consequently, Darwinism could be interpreted to support the idea that God is involved in "natural causes" *as well as* supernatural special actions.[381]

Even today, many Christians are not aware that both natural causes and miracles are supernatural. Without God maintaining the universe moment by moment, it would cease to exist–there would *be no* "natural causes" (Colossians 1:17; Hebrews 1:3). Yet the universe is *not* pre-determined in the sense that we are not able to make genuine choices. Where His rational creatures, including men and angels, are concerned, He has given us free will, the ability to actually change the course of events in both physical and transcendent reality *quite apart from* predetermined pathways. Thus we are morally accountable, and God allows us to experience the consequences of our genuine choices.

Around the end of the nineteenth century, *few* Christian theologians proposed that the *Bible* taught the earth was young. Seventh Day Adventists were predominant among the few who did. But by 1959, the one-hundredth anniversary of the publication of *The Origin*, evolution was being widely taught in schools *as fact*. At this point, Young Earth Creationism grew into a mainstream evangelical perspective, not only as a result of a particular interpretation of *Scripture*–including the conviction that the necessity of suffering and death in the evolutionary process *prior to human rebellion* seemed to conflict with the assertion that God is good–but also because Darwinism was essential to atheism, and a young earth would not allow enough time for evolution to have occurred.[382]

Yet, contrary to popular belief, it was *not* Darwin's theory of evolution which caused him to reject Christianity. Although by the time *The Origin of Species* was published, Darwin had rejected Christianity, he could not dispense with God. In *The Origin* he refers to material processes as "laws impressed on matter by the Creator," and could think of "no good reason why the views given in this volume should shock the religious feelings of anyone."[383] And frankly, today there are many Christians on each side of the evolutionary fence, and not a few sitting on it.

As for Darwin, while he did not totally dispense with the possibility of a supernatural First Cause, he apparently became a Deist or an agnostic in his final years. And in spite of the fact that the theory he developed *necessitated* the presence of pain and suffering, he gave the pervasiveness of human suffering, the doctrine of eternal suffering in hell, and the death of his daughter, as the primary reasons he had rejected the God of the *Bible*.[384]

Although he consulted with Asa Gray in an effort to resolve the problem of pain, he could not bring himself to accept Gray's assurance that pain had a Divine purpose.[385] Yet, he had greatly admired William Paley's argument for the existence of God based on evidence that the universe was designed, an argument which he had studied at Cambridge University. And at that time he had professed that Christianity provided "a future state of reward and punishment" which "gives order for confusion: makes the moral world of a piece with the natural."[386] However, he never seemed to grasp that God suffered on our behalf as He anticipated our rebellion and the loss we would incur, that Jesus suffered and died in order to restore our relationship with God, and that Divine suffering commends God's love to us and ultimately resolves the problem of pain! (Romans 5:8).

So, it seems that Charles Darwin ended up vehemently rejecting Paley's God–the God of the *Bible*. Still, we can hope he changed his mind in the last days of his life. After all, he was not unfamiliar with the teachings of *Scripture*. Because, when he left England aboard the Beagle . . . he had been preparing to become an Anglican minister![387] Yes, THERE'S ALWAYS MORE TO EVERY STORY.

The School of Suffering

<hr/>

The new normal will not eradicate the old. The new is simply an "in your face" version of the old – the old on steroids! If anyone who "keeps the whole law and yet stumbles at just one point is guilty of breaking all of it" (James 2:10 NIV), then we are *all* in deep trouble. In his book *The Revenge of Conscience: Politics and the Fall of Man*, J. Budziszewski, a professor of history and philosophy at the University of Texas, "shows how man's suppression of his knowledge of right and wrong corrupts his conscience and accelerates social collapse." He asserts that "a depraved *conscience* is the most destructive force in political life."[388] And certainly, the breathtaking changes in the moral vision of our culture do not bode well.

In a second book, *What We Can't Not Know*, Professor Budziszewski argues that because virtually all cultures over time and location share the same fundamental moral beliefs and practices, we are without excuse for denying that God has established the moral order.[389] This cultural phenomenon is known as "Natural Law" and is reputedly best summed up by the Ten Commandments. And Western Culture has developed a legal system based on *both* Natural Law and Judeo-Christian values.[390]

But that moral base has been eroding at an accelerating rate as secular humanism replaces these traditional foundational values with atheism, claiming moral superiority by promising to provide unfettered individual freedom. In effect, wrong becomes right!

Disrespect for parents, murder, adultery, dishonesty, theft, and coveting become "sacred rights."[391]

But it continues to be God's desire that those who oppose Him will change their minds and ask Him to change their hearts, and subsequently, every area of their lives, including their political philosophy. And in order to bring us to the point of faith, He places each of us in circumstances which teach us the truth of our situation. Contemplation of the creation assures us that God exists, and that we are therefore accountable to Him (Romans 1). Conscience informs us that right and wrong are absolute, not relative (Romans 2). And "Natural Law" further confirms that God's moral order must be honored if a culture is to thrive.

Our lives in this present age provide information and experiences which bear witness to the truth of *Scripture*, our dependence on God, our accountability to Him, the seriousness of sin, the restorative power of God's grace, and His loving offer to share His glory with us forever in his Eternal Kingdom (Romans 3 et al.).

In a world where sin and death reign, we must all deal with pain. Does the presence of pain mean that God is not loving? Pain warns us that something is wrong that needs to be made right. Whether physical, emotional, or spiritual, pain can motivate us to act in our own or others' best interests. "No pain, no gain" suggests that some goals can only be achieved the hard way. Parents and coaches can help their charges by allowing them to experience discomfort in order to achieve worthwhile goals. And when we are pursuing inappropriate goals, *natural consequences* may spur us to reevaluate our behaviors and change those goals.

With morality, however, there is a significant difference. Moral principles center in relationships—with God, self, others, and our environment—and violation of these principles *always* has negative consequences. Sin is missing the mark, falling short, failing to mirror the character and holiness of God. And the result, sooner or later, is pain. Yet as we reflect on the pain that our individual sins cause, as well as the pain due to natural causes in a world which is under

God's curse, we are given the opportunity to become "poor in spirit" (Matthew 5:3 NIV) and express a sincere desire to change. But inevitably we find that actually *making* this change is too much for us. (Matthew 5-7)

Here God offers to step in on our behalf, to free us from slavery to sin, to eliminate its power, penalty, and presence in our lives. He has arranged to forgive our sins, credit us with perfect righteousness, and transform us into people with Jesus' faultless humanity (Romans 8:28-30). For those who choose His Way "He will wipe every tear from their eyes. There will be no more death or mourning or crying or pain. . . ." (Revelation 21:4 NIV).

But it was not without cost to Himself that God made all this possible. Both Father and Son experienced pain as our salvation unfolded. God knew that we would turn away from Him. But though He doesn't need us, He nevertheless loves us and experienced the broken heart of a rejected parent *even prior to the creation of the universe*. And rather than reject us, He determined to reach out in love to restore that broken relationship. (Romans 8)

You see, Jesus was not only our morally perfect sin offering, but also completed His incarnational calling by personally experiencing human suffering from cradle to grave. What affirms God's love for us more than anything else is that Father and Son endured the *ultimate* pain when our sin, laid upon Jesus, caused Him to cry out to the Father, "Why have you forsaken me?" (Mark 15:34 AMP). So, as counter intuitive as it first appears, rather than thinking that God could not love us since He allows pain, we can rejoice that without pain Eternal life could not be ours! Yes, THERE'S ALWAYS MORE TO EVERY STORY.

The Strongman

The mythological Titan known as Atlas has become much of Western Culture's most familiar representative of unmatched strength. Atlas was sentenced to hold up the universe–the "celestial sphere"–for eternity after his side lost a war with the Olympic gods.[392] This winning side is the source of the name given to a real-life "war" of strength, speed, skill, and determination known as the Olympic Games. One of these contests pits the world's strongest men against each other in the sport of weightlifting. Natural ability, life experience, opportunity, training, and perseverance all combine with an extra something to produce a winner.

Some of us in the geriatric category will recall the ubiquity of advertisements in comic books and men's magazines for a program which would transform a "97-pound weakling" into a muscular marvel. Actually, the Charles Atlas program was a new twist in bodybuilding techniques and attracted many takers. The original 97-pound weakling was Charles Atlas himself, although when he developed his technique, he was Italian-born Angelo Siciliano, then living in Brooklyn. Statues of mythological strongmen such as Hercules in a local museum motivated him to bulk up. Young Angelo could not afford regular weight-training equipment, so he created a system, Dynamic-Tension, that pitted one muscle group against another.[393]

He eventually won recognition performing feats of strength in entertainment venues such as vaudeville, and posing for sculptures on buildings in Washington, D.C., and elsewhere. In contests held in Madison Square Garden he won the title of World's Most Handsome Man in 1921 and World's Most Perfectly Developed Man in 1922. In 1939, the AAU sponsored the first Mr. America contest, and from then on bodybuilding increased significantly in popularity, leading to international contests, notably Mr. Universe and Mr. Olympia. Today the most well-known bodybuilder is a seven-time winner of the Mr. Olympia title: Austrian-born Arnold Schwarzenegger.[394]

However, throughout the centuries the best-known true-life strongman in Western Culture has undoubtedly been an Israeli Judge by the name of Samson. The angel of the LORD told Samson's mother that she would bear a son "whose head is never to be touched by a razor because the boy is to be a Nazirite, dedicated to God from the womb. He will take the lead in delivering Israel from the hands of the Philistines" (Judges 13:5 NIV). Samson "grew and the LORD blessed him, and the Spirit of the LORD began to stir him" (Judges 13:24 and 25 NIV).

In spite of his many poor choices, he performed many amazing feats of strength and undermined Philistine authority. Eventually, however, his vulnerability to Delilah's wiles cost him his hair and his strength (Judges 16). Placed in a Philistine prison, with his eyes gouged out, Samson's strength was gradually restored as his hair grew back and he worked out grinding grain.

One day, the rulers and leading lights of Philistia gathered for a celebration in the temple of their god Dagon, because they believed Dagon had delivered Samson into their hands. Samson was brought in to perform for the crowd: three thousand people watching from the roof, and many gathered below. He eventually managed to have himself positioned between the two primary pillars of the temple. Then he prayed to God: "Sovereign LORD, remember me. Please, God, strengthen me just once more" (Judges 16:28 NIV). Then Samson pushed against the pillars, the temple roof fell, and Philistine rule was broken (Judges 16).

And although his name was not Samson, there was a *modern-day* strongman whose story in some ways parallels that of Samson. His weakness was not connected to his hair but to his kidneys. As a child, Paul was diagnosed with Bright's disease, a kidney disorder, and his parents were told that quite probably he would not live beyond eighteen. However, this would not be the case.[395]

As a freshman in high school, Paul was undersized, but his sister's husband suggested he start weightlifting. His brother-in-law helped him fabricate weights from junk and cement, and he bulked up and became a standout football player in high school and the one year he went to college.[396] But feeling that he was meant to focus on weightlifting, he dropped out of college to train under a world-class weightlifter and lifting coach.[397]

After breaking all his state's weightlifting records on his first try, Paul incurred a number of injuries, yet persisted in his efforts to develop his weight-lifting talent.[398] During his next year of competition, he broke so many records that numerous agents urged him to become a professional strongman. But he chose to remain an amateur in order to qualify for the World Championships and the Olympic Games.[399]

Paul was eventually chosen to join the United States weightlifting team and compete in a country engaged in a Cold War with the U.S. and priding itself in the superiority of its weightlifting program. It was a dual meet, a head-to-head battle during which the Russian heavyweight champion tied the Olympic record, pressing 330 pounds. But then, American heavyweight Paul Anderson called for a weight of 402.5 pounds! The Russian onlookers could not believe Anderson had done such a foolhardy thing and began to mock him. However, after he had successfully completed the lift, he had those Russian doubters calling him "a wonder of nature!"[400]

All along, Anderson's mother and her family had prayed for him, reminding him that God had made him special for a reason. But Anderson publicly credited his success to his diet, his exercise program, and the American way of life.[401] In 1956 Paul traveled to Australia to participate in the Olympics. Soon after arriving he suffered an inner ear infection that left him weakened. On the final day of the heavyweight competition Paul was trailing badly by the third and last lift, the clean-and-jerk. After failing on the first two of the three attempts allowed, he knew he was too weak to complete the lift on his last try.[402]

But like Samson, he turned to the One Who is the ultimate source of strength:

> Desperate, I lifted my first ever truly sincere prayer to God. "LORD, I know you've made me special and I've not given you credit. I want to be part of your Kingdom, and from here on out I'm making a real commitment. I'm not trying to make a deal, God, but I need your help to get this weight up."[403]

And—with God's help—Paul Anderson *did* get that weight up to win the gold medal in those 1956 Olympic Games![404]

After his Olympic victory, Anderson set out on a course of public appearances, but with a difference. He of course performed amazing feats of strength, but he also shared his story, giving credit to his Lord. Eventually, he and his wife, Glenda, established the Paul Anderson Youth Homes (PAYH), where troubled young men are introduced to the Savior, receive Christian counseling, and acquire valuable life skills.[405]

During his lifetime, Paul Anderson was acknowledged to be the strongest man who ever lived whose feats had been precisely documented. Who else could have completed a 6,270-pound backlift?[406] But more importantly, he would rather be remembered as an imitator of the One who holds all of the power lifting records in the universe and specializes in lifting lost souls to heights of eternal glory.

And by the way, remember fitness mogul Charles Atlas? *He* spent his last years keeping physically fit by running, and spiritually fit by reading the *Bible!*[407] Yes, THERE'S ALWAYS MORE TO EVERY STORY.

Ꚋ꙲ngues

People whose native language is English are sometimes unable to understand each other. This can be due to differences in the way the same words are pronounced, or to different words being used for the same things. Long Island University Reference Associate Robert Delaney explains:

> An accent refers only to the way words are pronounced . . ., while a dialect has its own grammar, vocabulary, syntax, and common expressions, as well as pronunciation rules that make it unique from other dialects of the same language.[408]

"Let's Call the Whole Thing Off," a song written by George and Ira Gershwin for a movie featuring Fred Astaire and Ginger Rogers, showcases different pronunciations:

> You say eether and I say eyether.

> You say neether and I say nyther.

> Eether, eyether, neether, nyther.

> Let's call the whole thing off!

> You like potato and I like potahto.

You like tomato and I like tomahto.

Potato, potahto, tomato, tomahto!

Let's call the whole thing off![409]

And it turns out that mere differences in pronunciation can also reflect social distinctions. In "Let's Call the Whole Thing Off," the second pronunciation of each pair of words is considered indicative of a higher social status.[410]

Within the United States, studies identify at least twenty-four American English dialects or subdialects. And further variants occur within these.[411] For instance, for those whose dialect is New England Eastern, Bar Harbor, Maine, becomes Bah Hahbuh as *r's* are replaced by *h's*. In Southeastern Louisiana, New Orleans becomes New Awlins if you are a native, while outsiders may mistakenly condense the two words into Nawlins.[412]

Then there's the matter of different words for the same thing. For those with a sweet tooth, depending on the dialect spoken in their region, doughnuts are dunkers, fatcakes, friedcakes, or olycooks, among others. In the Pacific Northwest, some residents refer to a big shot as a muckatymuck, a term used by Native Americans in the region. And it was here that the word *potluck* may have originated from the Native American term *potlatch*.

Things get even more complicated as we compare American English with Canadian, British, Australian, New Zealand, and other English dialects. Like the United States, each of these countries must deal with linguistic distinctions of its own. In England, these differences are entertainingly illustrated in the musical *My Fair Lady*. Phonetics professor Henry Higgins sets out to transform a woman who is a Cockney-dialect speaking member of working-class Londoners into someone who appears to be a proper member of high society. And she eventually passes the acid test due to her newly acquired refined behavior and Queen's English!

Along the way, audiences are exposed to the many variations in dialect which distinguish Cockney and Standard British English. In Cockney, *t* is often dropped: water becomes wa'er and city becomes ci'y. Rhyming slang reduces some phrases into a single word: "plate of meat" becomes "feet," and "apples and pears" becomes "stairs."[413]

All English-speaking countries have mutually recognizable pronunciations in their standard forms, although within each country there are a variety of dialects.[414] But even in standard form, words for the same thing can differ from country to country. If you order an icy pole in Australia, an iceblock in New Zealand, and an ice lolly in Britain, you will get the same thing as a popsicle in Canada and the US. An Esky in Australia is a chilly bin in New Zealand, a cool box in Britain, and an ice chest in America. English-speaking countries use both formal and informal words for "toilet." Among them are bathroom, washroom, restroom, lavatory, the loo, bog, Jacks, the John, and Dunny. If in doubt use "bathroom!"

In the first two books of C. S. Lewis's *Space Trilogy*, the main character is a philologist, Elwin Ransom, a person who studies the history of language and is prepared to decipher alien languages[415] His vocation serves him well in his encounters with intelligent life forms on other planets. As to the usefulness of philology in real life, the old television quiz show *I've Got a Secret* once featured a philologist who attempted to determine where people hailed from, based on their pronunciations and word choices. And he did amazingly well.

In a more serious vein, foreign spies and saboteurs whose native language is not English, train meticulously to master the behaviors and English dialect which would enable them to pass unsuspected in a particular English-speaking region. In 2010 a group of Russian agents were arrested by the FBI after they had successfully passed themselves off as ordinary US citizens. They attempted to develop relationships with Americans from whom they could obtain information advantageous to the Russian government. Eventually their deception was uncovered, and they were arrested and returned to Russia in exchange for some captive American agents.[416]

But imagine a situation where thousands of enemy troops were unmasked as a result of their inability to pronounce a particular word according to the rules of a particular dialect! Just such a scenario has played out in the Middle East. The Gileadites, who lived east of the Jordan River and were members of a clan within the Israeli tribe of Manasseh, had successfully repelled an attempted invasion by their Ammonite neighbors. However, members of the tribe of Ephraim, a tribe associated with the Gileadites, were incensed that they were not invited to help in the battle, although this accusation turned out to be a disputed claim. Nevertheless, they were so angry at their brother Israelis that they went to war against them and were defeated. (Judges 11:1-12:4)

As Ephraimite warriors fled back toward their tribal land they had to cross the Jordan River. Without distinctive military uniforms it was nearly impossible to tell the fleeing Ephraimites from the victorious Gileadites by sight. So the Gileadites patrolled the fords of the Jordan, asking those attempting to cross to pronounce the word meaning "torrent of water." If they said "Sibboleth" instead of "Shibboleth," their names were added to the list of 42,000 Ephraimites slain during the conflict! (Judges 12:4-6 NIV). Yes, THERE'S ALWAYS MORE TO EVERY STORY.

Torah

+ ✦✦✦✦ +

"Torah" commonly refers to the Five Books of Moses, the first five books of the *Bible*. But to Orthodox Jews, Torah is a great deal more. It is an attitude, it is a way of thinking, it is in fact the sum total of all that distinguishes Israel as a people. It is the Book, it is the people of the Book, it is the land of the Book. And the Book commands the people to dwell in the land. And at last Joe was going home.[417]

Joe was familiar with the story of Abraham–how God had shown him the land which would one day be occupied by a nation formed of his descendants. But that occupancy had turned out to be an on-again off-again affair. Yet, the determination to return to the land had always been of paramount importance to any exile who kept alive the vision of the Land of Promise. Moses had. Jeremiah had. Nehemiah and Ezra had. And even after the devastation of Jerusalem in 70 CE (Common Era) smashed all hope that the zealots could secure Jewish independence from Rome, many of the rabbis and other leaders continued to urge the people to never lose sight of their indissoluble association with the land.

But not all of the children of Israel maintained this allegiance to the land. Soon after the fall of Jerusalem in 70 AD, the Jewish colony in the former area of Babylonia–consisting of those who had lived there ever since Nebuchadnezzar had exiled Jews to Babylon, plus those who had fled there in the wake of Roman reprisals against those seeking independence–was the largest body of Jews anywhere, including the land of Israel. Many of these diasporic Jews settled more or less comfortably into their surroundings, and even among those who staunchly maintained their Jewish ways, there were large numbers who felt they could function as Jews just as well in foreign lands as in Israel.[418]

Over the centuries that followed, Jews were further dispersed throughout the world. Some were absorbed into alien cultures; but others persistently clung to their Jewish heritage, though developing diverse forms of Jewish expression.

Even today there is great variation among Jewish leaders as to the role which the land plays in Israeli life. Nevertheless, among those who see no necessity for they themselves returning to the land, there are many who view the reestablishment of the Nation of Israel to be of tremendous significance to all Jews everywhere who cherish their Jewish identity. After all, was it not a part of Torah? Yet since not all Jewish people are Orthodox nor place special value upon returning to Israel themselves, "Jewish identity" may be difficult to agree upon.[419]

But all who derive their Jewish identity from Torah look longingly for the Messiah to appear in Israel, to liberate them from those powers which would debase or destroy them, and to establish Israel's place forever as peacekeeper among the nations. So it is that many of the children of Israel long to return to the land of their roots, their faith, their traditions, their destiny.[420]

And Joe had long ago made up his mind to return. He had been in exile long enough. Generations of his family had lived and died outside of Israel; many of his people had longed desperately to return to the land but had lacked opportunity or been denied exit visas. But Joe was certain that his opportunity would eventually come, and his certainty helped keep alive the hopes of his people. Anticipating that day, he had made careful plans for his departure. And he was prepared to leave on a moment's notice.

Finally that moment had arrived, and he was going home—after an absence of four-hundred years. For you see, Joe had left home *before* Israel had even become a nation, *before* the Torah had even been written. And now he was returning in the company of those who would establish Israeli control over Palestine for the very *first* time. At last Joe–that is, Joe's–Joseph's–carefully embalmed body–was leaving Egypt and going home. Yes, THERE'S ALWAYS MORE TO EVERY STORY.

Vibrations

We live in a vibrant world–both figuratively and literally. In fact, if we are deprived of the sound vibrations in our environment, we will quickly become disoriented. Known as "the quietest place on earth," an anechoic (no echoes) chamber not only eliminates sound from the outside but also prevents sounds produced by an occupant's body (heartbeat, lungs, etc.) from creating an echo. [421] Under these conditions an occupant quickly loses the ability to orient and balance their body in space, and eventually begins hallucinating. No one is able to tolerate the silence for long![422]

Vibrations are, indeed, essential to our lives. The word "vibrant" in this context means "full of energy and enthusiasm, high spirited, full of life."[423] Moreover, some scientists are proposing that all matter consists of submicroscopic *vibrating strings* which vary in physical properties according to differences in their vibrations. The ultimate hope is that "String Theory" will account for all physical phenomena.[424]

Vibrations can be pictured as waves, the height and frequency of a wave representing the amount of energy a particular vibration possesses. In the beginning, the Word–the Word Who was and is God–spoke the universe into existence, setting its vibrational aspects in motion (John 1:1-3). The vibrations of our DNA and proteins are essential to their biological functions.[425] And those whose spiritual vibrations resonate with the Spirit of God experience what the *Bible* calls abundant life (John 10:10).

Vibrations are produced in many different ways and may be beneficial or destructive. The vibrations produced as we create sounds with our bodies can build up or tear down. You may recall the scene in *The Adventures of Tintin: The Secret of the Unicorn*, when a world-renowned opera singer shatters a glass display case when she hits a particular note.[426] In this instance, the vibration rate of that note equaled the "natural frequency" of the glass (the rate at which it vibrates when not forced to vibrate differently). This "resonance" increased the shaking in the glass to the point that it disintegrated.[427]

Much more importantly, the *Bible* reminds us that the vibrations we produce *when we speak* convey meanings which can *also* build up or tear down:

> [N]o human being can tame the tongue. It is a restless evil, full of deadly poison. With the tongue we praise our Lord and Father, and with it we curse human beings, who have been made in God's likeness. Out of the same mouth come praise and cursing. (James 3:8-10 NIV)

Because of the potential for damage which vibrations possess, architects and engineers must take special precautions when designing structures. "Galloping Gertie," the first bridge built over the Tacoma Narrows in Washington State, and the third-longest suspension bridge in the world at the time, never could resist the temptation to shimmy in the wind and traffic. Engineering flaws and a steady but not particularly powerful wind eventually caused the bridge to tear itself apart.[428]

In addition to dealing with wind, earthquakes, and other forces of nature which generate destructive vibrations, designers must also anticipate the effects of humanly generated vibrations such as those produced by machinery or even our footsteps! Such lesser vibrations can actually add enough vibrational energy to that of other more powerful vibrations to push a structure past its breaking point.[429]

Today, when a structure such as a high-rise building has outlived its usefulness, knowledge of the vibrational impact of explosives comes in handy. Foremost in taking these structures down safely with the least possible use of explosives is Controlled Demolition, Inc., a decades old business of the Loizeaux family. (Another Loizeaux family enterprise was Loizeaux Brothers, Inc., a publishing company that printed Christian literature, including the works of H. A. Ironside.) Knowing exactly where to place explosive charges to bring a structure down is Controlled Demolition's specialty.[430]

But demolishing a formidable structure in ages past would have been extremely tedious, perhaps not even worth the effort. Nevertheless, might it have been possible to flatten such a structure *rapidly* without the requisite knowledge and technology available today? For example, could a combination of vibrations created by the continuous sounding of horns, shouting of voices, and stamping of marching feet provide the last straw needed to demolish a structure which had already been weakened over time?

Certainly God more often accomplishes His will in the physical realm by letting "nature run its course." And perhaps that was the case after the people of Israel circled the ancient walls of Jericho for the final time, allowing their conquest of the Promised Land to begin.[431] Yes, THERE'S ALWAYS MORE TO EVERY STORY.

Water World

✦ ✦✦✦✦✦ ✦

Scientists call Earth the *water planet*. Astronauts report that the most outstanding feature of Earth from space is the water covering seventy-five percent of its surface. Oceans, lakes, rivers, and vast icefields also impress those viewing them from *within* the envelope of gases surrounding our planetary home. Even that envelope–our atmosphere–contains water: invisible vapor, liquid rain, and solid snow or hail.

Water is essential to all living things. It's involved in many bodily functions, and in general we can live for about three weeks without food, but only one week without water. Over ninety-seven percent of the accessible sources of water are salty.[432] As the *Rhyme of the Ancient Mariner* reminds us, for those who ply the oceans, there is "water, water, everywhere, but not a drop to drink."[433]

Many of today's scientists propose that as the Earth formed out of dust and gases strewn in space, it was eventually covered in molten lava. As the lava cooled our planet gradually accumulated water, primarily, according to this theory, as a result of water-bearing asteroids strikes.[434] Earth retains the water it now possesses because the upper regions of our atmosphere are so cold that water vapor turns solid and eventually falls back to the surface rather than escaping into space. In fact, water is the only substance on earth that can exist as a liquid, solid, or gas in nature.[435]

Much of Earth's freshwater is tied up in glacial ice, predominantly in Antarctica and Greenland. So, it is lakes, rivers, and groundwater that provide most of the water we use. And that water is replenished by atmospheric precipitation of rain, snow, and ice. Water in the atmosphere is in turn replenished by evaporation of water from the oceans and other bodies of water. During this process, any salts are left behind; consequently, the water in the atmosphere is freshwater.[436]

The constant circulation of freshwater between earth and sky is known as the *hydrologic cycle*. Although their purpose was to illustrate God's provision for the well-being of living things, the nature of this cycle can be deduced from many passages of *Scripture* written well before a scientific explanation was available. Among other biblical assertions that were at first rejected but eventually shown to be true is the claim that precipitation of atmospheric water is more than sufficient to renew the freshwater taken from lakes, rivers, and groundwater (see Ecclesiastes 1:7, among other passages). Prior to scientific verification of this assertion, it was thought that sources of water deeper than groundwater were needed to provide the amount of water required.[437]

In *Scripture*, water is associated with both life and death. In the Garden of Eden, the tree of life was watered by a river. Beyond the Garden, lack of rainfall brought droughts which resulted in loss of life, whereas living water–running, as opposed to stagnant, water–brought abundant life. *New Testament* water baptism speaks of identifying with Christ in His death and in His resurrection, symbolizing the Christian's "new birth." Jesus Himself offered a Samaritan woman "living water" saying that "whoever drinks the water I give them will never thirst. Indeed, the water I give them will become in them a spring of water welling up to eternal life." (John 4:10 and 14 NIV)

The alternative to eternal life is the final judgment, perhaps most memorably illustrated in the *Old Testament* by the Flood of Noah's time. Certainly, there is disagreement even among Christians as to whether the Noahic Flood was merely a local phenomenon or a world-wide event. Of course, skeptics tend to dismiss it altogether, considering it merely a myth. However, Genesis 1 describes an earth covered in liquid water which was subsequently interspersed with dry land. If the earth had a smooth surface, the waters of the ocean would cover it to a depth of one and two-thirds miles. But to entirely cover an earth featuring mountains and other highlands would require considerably more water than rain could supply.[438] Actually, the *Bible* states that:

> all the springs of the great deep burst forth, and the floodgates of the heavens were opened. And rain fell on the earth forty days and forty nights. . . . [A]ll the high mountains under the entire heavens were covered. (Genesis 7:11, 12, and 19 NIV)

Skeptics point to the lack of an adequate source of water to account for a global flood. But recent scientific studies suggest that, between two-hundred fifty and over four-hundred miles below Earth's surface, there are vast pockets of water which altogether amount to as much as *three times* the water in all the world's oceans![439] And if "all the springs of the great deep burst forth," they would easily supply enough additional water to account for a worldwide flood. Yes, THERE'S ALWAYS MORE TO EVERY STORY.

What's in a Name?

✦✦✦✦✦✦

Futurists have traditionally been divided in their opinions regarding the ultimate fate of this planet and the human race. On one hand, doomsayers project the horrors of a nuclear holocaust, with those of us not killed outright facing the prospect of inevitable death from radiation poisoning, plague, starvation, or any of numerous other causes linked to the ravages of a nuclear winter. Meanwhile, humanists envision a world in which men have overcome the pride and selfishness which trace to their animal ancestry, and have united to create a utopia in which reason and man's better instincts prevail, in which artificial intelligence and the myriad other fruits of technology enable us to extend human life indefinitely and set out to the stars.

One of C.S. Lewis's most famous characters, the senior demon Screwtape, was equally anxious to promote a grossly cynical or naively optimistic view of the future. *The Screwtape Letters* documents Screwtape's efforts to instruct his inexperienced nephew Wormwood in the fundamental principles of deviltry. At one point, Screwtape informs Wormwood that "tortured fear and stupid confidence [regarding the future] are both desirable states of mind" to encourage in their human victims.[440] Either view of the future is acceptable as long as it prevents men from seeing the truth.[441]

Certainly, the *Bible* indicates that things are going to get worse before they get better. And, interestingly enough, the name which Lewis chose for Screwtape's nephew is a word which is associated in the *Bible* with the bitterness of suffering and calamity experienced by those who reject God. For example, in the book of *Jeremiah*, the LORD says concerning false prophets, "I am going to feed them wormwood and make them drink poisonous water. For from the prophets of Jerusalem Pollution has gone forth into all the land." (Jeremiah 23:15 NASB 1995)

Unfortunately, in our day, pollution of the environment has become, for many, a more pressing issue than pollution of the soul. And *Bible* scholars are marshaling growing evidence that some of the end-time judgments depicted so vividly in the *Scriptures* will in fact be self-inflicted. Even the violent demise of the present heavens and earth—"the heavens will pass away with a roar and the elements will be destroyed with intense heat, and the earth and its works will be burned up" (II Peter 3:10 NASB 1995)—is something which man can now begin to imagine *himself* initiating!

But, even *apart* from the weapons of mass destruction which have accumulated since scientists first unleashed the awesome power of the atom decades ago—along with the accompanying problem of nuclear waste—we are *quite capable of inflicting irreparable damage* on the biosphere, the thin layer of air, water, soil and living things unique to our planet. While the Industrial Revolution of an earlier century, and subsequent technological breakthroughs, have enabled us to substantially diminish some of the suffering and toil with which we have contended since the *Edenic Fall*, they have also enabled us to rapidly deplete resources, introduce toxic wastes into the environment, increase cancer rates, extinguish species, and generally disrupt creation's crucial balance.

All of this has given "one-worlders" compelling grounds for their contention that a central world authority is the only means of effectively resolving those problems which increasingly threaten our survival on this planet. However, the *Bible* says that not only will men be unable to resolve their current difficulties, but those troubles will be greatly multiplied as Christ's return nears. Ungodly men will drink the bitter cup of Divine judgment, a cup filled with wormwood! (Matthew 24)

To what extent man's technology will be responsible for some of the catastrophic events which culminate this present age we cannot be certain, but there is ample room for speculation. In the eighth chapter of *Revelation*, for instance, the Apostle John describes a number of end-time judgments which are at least partially explainable in terms of man-made causes. Take the third judgment, for example:

> [A] great star fell from heaven, burning like a torch, and it fell on a third of the rivers and on the springs of waters; and the name of the star is called Wormwood; and a third of the waters became wormwood; and many men died from the waters, because they were made bitter. (Revelation 8:10 and 11 NASB 1977)

John could easily have been describing a non-military nuclear event, such as the meltdown and explosion of an electricity-generating atomic energy facility, the consequent contamination of rain and groundwater, and the inevitable loss of life which would result. The events which occurred in 1986 in the former Soviet Union near the populous city of Kiev comprised just such a scenario and have perhaps provided us with a preview of things to come—might even be a partial fulfillment of prophecy.

Whatever the case, many throughout the Soviet Union excitedly discussed the possibilities. For you see, they knew that the Russian version of the Ukrainian word for *wormwood*, the bitter drink which symbolizes God's judgment, is the Russian name for a hitherto little-known Ukrainian town . . . Chernobyl![442] Yes, THERE'S ALWAYS MORE TO EVERY STORY.

Who Is There to Thank?

T-Day rolls around every November, just as X-Day comes each December. We know why the X has taken the place of Christmas in the latter: after all, we're no longer a Christian nation and wouldn't want to violate the separation of church and state! But even in a secular nation, who could be offended by a day of thanksgiving, other than the turkey?

Yes, consistent atheists could object because they claim that everything is predetermined by the impersonal forces of physical cause-and-effect. True, it would only make sense to thank the electromagnetic force, the strong nuclear force, the weak nuclear force, and gravitation, if each of these four fundamental forces of the physical universe had a way of perceiving gratitude. And the "good luck" to which people often refer when expressing gratitude for favorable outcomes is equally incapable of appreciating it.

However, phrases such as "luck of the draw" and "lucky stars" seem to suggest a realization that there's something *more* than physical forces at work. And quite apart from the matter of impersonal forces, even consistent atheists usually feel it's appropriate to give thanks to whomever they perceive as contributing to favorable outcomes in their lives: themselves, other persons, and intelligent animals such as dogs or horses who can appreciate and acknowledge gratitude. It's the socially fitting thing to do in our culture, regardless of one's rejection or acceptance of transcendent reality, of the existence of God.

Nevertheless, most people actually *do* profess belief in transcendent reality, that there is more than just the physical universe to wrap our minds around. Whatever form it takes, it's not something that scientists can directly observe and analyze. They can observe the *effects* it has on the material world, including human beings. But they cannot observe the immaterial, transcendent, causes at work. From physical data they may draw inferences that favor either an atheistic or a theistic viewpoint, but in the end, transcendence must be *revealed* to us by the source of that transcendence.

The orthodox Christian view is that human beings are created in the image of God, enabling us to be "holy, loving, just, good, merciful, gracious, faithful, truthful, patient, and wise."[443] It is through these attributes that God reveals the true nature of reality to each and every individual person: Spirit to spirit.

Thus, we learn that every aspect of our being has been tainted by sin. God's image in us has been distorted and we can do nothing to restore it. But God can—and is willing to do so: "But thank God! He gives us victory over sin and death through our Lord Jesus Christ." (I Corinthians 5:57 NLT) And God is always available to receive our thanks. What's more, He often works in truly amazing ways in meriting our thanksgiving.

The English slave trader best-known to European and American Christians became a slave himself before being delivered from captivity and from his slavery to sin. John Newton summarized his experience in a song titled "Amazing Grace." It powerfully expresses his reasons for being thankful. And having been both a slave trader and slave himself, he knew that God would have him support William Wilberforce's campaign to abolish the slave trade in the British Empire, and Newton lived to see this trade finally abolished in 1807.[444]

But up until then, the English were actively involved in the slave trade in many different areas. Early in the 1600s, a group of young Native Americans were tricked aboard a British trading vessel and taken to Europe where they were sold as slaves in Spain. However, one of these young men managed to escape to England. He lived in London, became fluent in the English language, and absorbed knowledge of English culture.[445]

In 1619 he was employed by a British trade mission as an interpreter on a trip to New England. The next year, the trade mission was chased out of the territory by the local Wampanoag tribe, and the mission's interpreter, Tisquantum, was captured and forced to live with the Wampanoag.[446]

During the winter of that year, a recently arrived group of English settlers had suffered great hardships, including the loss of forty-five of the original one-hundred-and-two colonists due to malnutrition, disease, and other causes.[447] For their new settlement, these colonists had actually chosen a site which had previously been occupied by members of Tisquantum's Patuxet tribe, which, except for Tisquantum, had been wiped out by diseases introduced by Europeans.[448]

Meanwhile, the Wampanoag were trying to decide how to respond to the presence of these foreigners. After much consideration, they decided to approach the colonists on friendly terms and seek to establish a mutually beneficial relationship. It's difficult to imagine the Englishers' surprise and elation when out of the forest wilderness stepped a native American tribesman who spoke excellent English, was familiar with their culture, and offered life-preserving help![449]

In the fall of that year, "as an expression of their gratitude, the Pilgrims invited [Tisquantum] and around 90 Wampanoag to join them in a celebration of their first successful harvest in what they called the 'New World.'"[450] Along with sharing corn and squash which Tisquantum—more familiarly known as Squanto—had introduced to the colonists and they had grown successfully in preparation for their second winter, the native Americans and Puritans (later called Pilgrims) shared wild turkey, waterfowl, venison, lobster, clams, and fruit—perhaps even including cranberries.[451]

And of course, the Puritans were not only thankful to Squanto and the Wampanoag, but as Christians, they especially thanked

God for the miraculous way in which He had lovingly provided for their survival! You see, the ship on which they had crossed the ocean, the Mayflower, was originally scheduled to enter the Hudson River below present-day New York City. Unless they encountered European traders in that area, and enlisted their advice, they would be on their own, unable to readily communicate with any Native American neighbors. But rough seas forced the crew to land farther north, on the tip of Cape Cod, and the settlers subsequently chose to establish their community–eventually called Plymouth Plantation–due west across Cape Cod Bay, on that site formerly occupied by Squanto's relatives.[452] And that is where Squanto emerged from the wilderness and mediated their survival in the English language!

When Squanto lay dying a year later, he asked William Bradford, the first governor of Plymouth Plantation, to "pray for him, that he might go to the Englishmen's God in heaven, and bequeathed [many] of his things to . . . his English friends," whom he loved and who considered his death a "great loss."[453]

How great a loss was expressed by Governor Bradford when he called Squanto "a special instrument sent of God."[454] And surely he was! Yes, THERE'S ALWAYS MORE TO EVERY STORY.

Zodiac

We humans have always been fascinated by the stars and other celestial objects, including the moon and planets. In antiquity, these objects began to be worshipped as gods. Of course, our sun, a medium-sized star known as a "yellow dwarf," took priority. The sun god was given such names as Helios, Apollo, and Ra. Certainly, the earliest humans soon recognized their dependence on the sun to provide light and warmth, causing some of them to deify it.[455] Thus, in the *Bible*, God warns the Israelites:

> [B]eware that you do not raise your eyes toward heaven and see the sun and the moon and the stars, all the host of heaven, and let yourselves be led astray and worship them and serve them, [mere created bodies] which the LORD your God has allotted to [serve and benefit] all the peoples under the whole heaven. (Deuteronomy 4:19 AMP).

And like the Israelites, we are all prone to worship the creation—especially ourselves—rather than our Creator. Even today, the worship of the "host of heaven" is far from being relegated to the scrap heap. The fact is that many people in both third world and developed countries *persist* in looking to *astrology* to provide guidance concerning their personality, choices, and future. Some claim that astrology is *not* a religion because it's based on direct sensory observations. However, the claim that it's scientific begs the question: it assumes that since stars form specific patterns and move in predictable paths, they *must* provide objective data essential to our well-being.

It's one thing to observe the physical aspects of the universe, including the patterns and movements of celestial objects. But it's quite another to claim that those aspects reveal detailed insight into the course of one's life. Obviously, to account for such knowledge, a power other than some part of material reality must exist and must be taken by *faith, not sight.* Thus, astrology *should* definitely be categorized as a religion, and even those who only dabble in it do so at their own risk.[456]

The particular portion of the "host of heaven" which is central to astrology is found in a narrow band along the path of the sun as viewed from Earth. This band, known as the zodiac, contains the so-called signs of the zodiac. In modern astrology, these signs are prominent groupings of stars—constellations—which bear names dating back to ancient times.

Although many constellations are located in the zodiac, the traditional Western version of astrology deals with twelve. For millennia these twelve (with common English equivalents) have been known as Aries (the Ram), Taurus (the Bull), Gemini (the Twins), Cancer (the Crab), Leo (the Lion), Virgo (the Virgin), Libra (the Scales), Scorpio (the Scorpion), Sagittarius (the Archer), Capricorn (the Goat), Aquarius (the Water-Bearer), and Pisces (the Fishes).[457]

Absolutely, Christianity rejects astrology in its idolatrous form. But in the following *Bible* passage perhaps God pointed out something *other than* the vastness of the starry host when He told Abraham to observe the night sky:

> Look now toward heaven, and tell [list] the stars,
> if thou be able to number them [enumerate them,
> list them in order]: and he said unto him, So shall
> thy seed be. And he believed in the LORD; and

he counted it to him for righteousness." (Genesis 15:5 and 6 KJV; brackets based on Duane Edward Spencer's book *Mazzaroth*[458])

Could this be what the very first chapter in the *Bible* means when it points out that the sun, moon, and stars are to serve as *signs*, as well as to measure off seasons, days, and years (Genesis 1:14)? Certainly, *signs in the starry heavens including "his star"* were what persuaded the wise men—the magi—to seek out and worship the newborn King of the Jews.

Psalm 19 suggests that not only are the heavens a general testament to the existence and greatness of God, but are also a means by which He communicates knowledge:

> The heavens declare the glory of God; the skies proclaim the work of his hands. Day after day they pour forth speech; night after night they reveal knowledge. They have no speech, they use no words; no sound is heard from them. Yet their voice goes out into all the earth, their words to the ends of the world. In the heavens God has pitched a tent for the sun. It is like a bridegroom coming out of his chamber, like a champion rejoicing to run his course. It rises at one end of the heavens and makes its circuit to the other; nothing is deprived of its warmth. (Psalm 19:1-6 NIV)

Could the knowledge thus revealed include information regarding specific events? What if the original names of the constellations and individual stars in the zodiac actually "preach" the Gospel! After all, when the Apostle Paul refers to God's promise to Abraham, he makes sure his readers know that:

> Scripture foresaw that God would justify the Gentiles by faith, and *announced the gospel in advance to Abraham*: "All nations will be blessed through you" (Galatians 3:8 NIV; italics mine).

> The promises were spoken to Abraham and to his seed. Scripture does not say "and to seeds," meaning many people, but "and to your seed," meaning one person, who is Christ. (Galatians 3:16 NIV).

Surely Paul is referring to God's promise to Abraham as found in Genesis 5:5-6, which could be paraphrased to sum up the Gospel: Abraham was credited with righteousness as a result of his faith in what Christ would accomplish, as revealed in the message Abraham read in the stars!

There is certainly ample biblical evidence that the sun is a symbol of Christ, the heavenly Bridegroom of the church who runs His race against the background stars of the zodiac. One reference is Psalm 19:4-6 considered in light of the redemptive work of Jesus. And it is unquestionably He Who provides righteousness for those who place their trust in Him. But if indeed the signs of the zodiac present the Gospel, with which constellation would the Good News begin?

Since the Gospel is set in motion by the Incarnation, and continues eternally with the return of Christ as the Lion of the Tribe of Judah, its portrayal in the zodiac must seemingly begin with Virgo and end with Leo. The implications of this possibility are well-worth considering, and the supporting details persuasive! And you can check all this out in Emmaus Bible College Faculty Emeritus Kenneth C. Fleming's book, *God's Voice in the Stars: Zodiac Signs and Bible Truth*.[459] Because yes, THERE'S ALWAYS MORE TO EVERY STORY.

Endnotes

1 Wikipedia. "James Bartley." Last accessed November 11, 2021, https://en.wikipedia.org/wiki/James_Bartley.

2 Ibid.

3 Bambi Turner, "Has a whale ever swallowed someone alive?" HowStuffWorks, Updated: Apr 14, 2021, https://animals.howstuffworks.com/animal-facts/whale-swallowed-someone-alive.htm.

4 Rose Eveleth, "Could a Whale Accidentally Swallow You? It Is Possible," *Smithsonian*, February 25, 2013, Last accessed June 19, 2021, https://www.smithsonianmag.com/smart-news/could-a-whale-accidentally-swallow-you-it-is-possible-26353362/.

5 Jennifer Hile, "Great White Shark Attacks: Defanging the Myths," *National Geographic*, January 23, 2004, Last accessed June 19, 2021, https://www.nationalgeographic.com/animals/article/great-white-shark-myths.

6 Richard Woolveridge, "Did a 19th-century sailor get swallowed by a sperm whale and survive?" *Australian Geographic*, History & Culture, March 2, 2017, Last accessed June 19, 2021, https://www.australian geographic.com.au/topics/history-culture/2017/03/did-a-19th-century-sailor-get-swallowed-by-a-sperm-whale-and-survive/.

7 Edward B. Davis, "A Whale of a Tale: Fundamentalist Fish Stories," *Perspectives on Science and Christian Faith*, American Scientific Affiliation, December 1991, Last accessed June 20, 2021, https://www.asa3.org /ASA/PSCF/1991/PSCF12-91Davis.html.

8 Wikipedia. "Electromagnetic radiation." Last accessed June 20, 2021, https://en.wikipedia.org/wiki/Electromagnetic_radiation.

9 EarthSky editors, "How many stars can you see?" Last accessed June 20, 2021, https://earthsky.org/astronomy-essentials/how-many-stars-could-you-see-on-a-clear-moonless-night/.

10 The European Space Agency, "How many stars are there in the Universe?" Science & Exploration, Last accessed June 20, 2021, https://www.esa. int/Science_Exploration/Space_Science/Herschel/How_many_stars_ are_there_in_the_Universe.

11 Karl Hille, editor, "Hubble Reveals Observable Universe Contains 10 Times More Galaxies Than Previously Thought," *Galaxies*, NASA, Last updated: Aug 6, 2017, Last accessed June 20, 2021, https://www.nasa. gov/feature/goddard/2016/hubble-reveals-observable-universe-contains-10-times-more-galaxies-than-previously-thought.

12 Bob Berman, "The everlasting question: more sand or stars?" *Astronomy*, January 23, 2019, Last Accessed June 20, 2021, https:// astronomy.com/ magazine/bob-berman/2019/01/more-sand-or-stars.

13 Richard B.Larson and Volker Bromm, "The First Stars in the Universe," *Scientific American*, January 19, 2009, Last accessed June 20, 2021, https://www.scientificamerican.com/article/the-first-stars-in-the-un/.

14 Elizabeth Landau, "Symphony of Stars: The Science of Stellar Sound Waves," Exoplanet Exploration, NASA, July 30, 2018, Last accessed June 20, 2021, https://exoplanets.nasa.gov/news/1516/ symphony-of-stars-the-science-of-stellar-sound-waves/.

15 Fraser Cain, "What Are The Different Types of Stars?" Universe Today, Space and Astronomy News, January 28, 2009, Last accessed June 20, 2021, https://www.universetoday.com/24299/types-of-stars/.

16 Wikipedia. "Zoroastrianism." Last accessed June 20, 2021, https://en. wikipedia.org/wiki/Zoroastrianism.

17 Ibid.

18 Wikipedia. "Friedrich Nietzsche." Last accessed June 20, 2021, https:// en.wikipedia.org/wiki/Friedrich_Nietzsche.

19 Alexander S. King, "Nietzsche's Death of God: Why Zarathustra?" StackExchange, Philosophy, February 9, 2016, Last accessed June 21, 2021, https://philosophy.stackexchange.com/ questions/32034/ nietzsches-death-of-god-why-zarathustra.

20 Classicfm, "This is the most epic musical 'sunrise' ever written." Music, Last accessed June 21, 2021, https://www.classic fm.com/ composers/ strauss/music/also-sprach-zarathustra-sunrise/.

21 Wikipedia. "Also sprach Zarathustra." Last accessed June 20, 2021, https://en.wikipedia.org/wiki/Also_sprach_Zarathustra.

22 Eternalized, "Friedrich Nietzsche – 10 Key Ideas," April 29, 2021, Last accessed August 14, 2021, https://eternalisedofficial.com/2021/04/29/ friedrich-nietzsche-10-key-ideas/.

23 Wikipedia. "Epiphany (holiday)." Last accessed June 21, 2021, https://
en.wikipedia.org/wiki/Epiphany_(holiday).

24 Tanya Pai, "The 12 Days of Christmas: The story behind the holiday's
most annoying carol," Vox, December 1, 2020, Last accessed August 5,
2021, https://www. vox.com/21796404/12-days-of-christmas-explained.

25 Ray Bohlin, "The Star of Bethlehem from a Christian View," Probe, Last
accessed August 14, 2021, https://probe.org/the-star-of-bethlehem/.

26 Wikipedia. "Biblical Magi." Last accessed June 21, 2021, https://en.
wikipedia.org/wiki/Biblical_Magi.

27 Guy Winch, "5 Ways Emotional Pain Is Worse Than Physical
Pain," Psychology Today, July 20, 2014, Last accessed July 12, 2021,
https://www.psychologytoday.com/us/blog/the-squeaky-wheel/
201407/5-ways-emotional-pain-is-worse-physical-pain.

28 Joni and Friends, "Transforming Lives through Joni's House," Last
accessed June 21, 2021, https://www.joniandfriends.org/.

29 Newbigin, Lesslie. 1986. Foolishness to the Greeks (Grand Rapids: Wm.
B. Eerdmans Publishing Company), 29-33.

30 McLuhan, Marshall. 1964. Understanding Media: The Extensions of Man
(Cambridge: The MIT Press).

31 Schaeffer, Francis A. 1970. "A Substantial Healing," in Pollution and the
Death of Man (Wheaton: Tyndale House Publishers).

32 Newbigin, op. cit.

33 Anxiety & Depression Association of America, "Bipolar Disorder,"
Last accessed June 21, 2021, https://adaa.org/understanding-anxiety/
co-occurring-disorders/bipolar-disorder.

34 Access Community Health Network, "3 Most Common Mental
Health Disorders in America," May 16, 2019, Last accessed
July 12, 2021, https://www.achn.net/about-access/whats-new/
health-resources/3-most-common-mental-health-disorders-in-america/.

35 Genesight, "Managing Multiple Diagnoses of Mental Illness,"
Last accessed June 21, 2021, https://genesight.com/blog/ patient/
managing-multiple-mental-illnesses/.

36 Online Psychology Degree Guide, "15 Scariest Mental Disorders of
All Time," Last accessed June 21, 2021, https://www.onlinepsychology
degree.info/terrifying-mental-disorders/.

37 Ibid.

38 Amber Blaize, "Boanthropy – One of the weirdest disorders you've never
heard of," Our Weird & Wonderful World, June 8, 2020, Last accessed
August 9, 2021, https://medium.com/our-weird-wonderful-world/

boanthropy-one-of-the-weirdest-disorders-youve-never-heard-of-cd8f65cb53b4.

39 Shahpesandy, Homayun, M.D., MSc., PhD. 2019. "Psychology and philosophy of the human mind: Theologico-philosophical perspectives of Sanai, Ghazali, Rumi, Razi and Avicenna about the human spirit," Paper presented at the 19th WPA World Congress of Psychiatry, Lisbon, August 21-24, 2019, https://www.researchgate.net/publication/335685553_Psychology_and_philosophy_of_the_human_mind_Theologicophilosophical_perspectives_of_Sanai_Ghazali_Rumi_Razi_and_Avicenna_about_the_human_spirit.

40 Wikipedia. "Avicenna." Last accessed June 21, 2021, https://en.wikipedia.org/wiki/Avicenna.

41 Shahpesandy, op. cit.

42 Stanford University, "A History of the Heart," Stanford History Class, Last accessed June 21, 2021, https://web.stanford.edu/class/history13/earlyscience lab/ body/heartpages/heart.html.

43 Rod Brouhard, "How Long Does Brain Activity Last After Cardiac Arrest?" VeryWellHealth, First Aid, Updated on January 26, 2020, https://www.verywellhealth. com/brain-activity-after-cardiac-arrest-1298429.

44 Ali M. Alshami, "Pain: Is It All in the Brain or the Heart?" National Library of Medicine, National Institutes of Health, November 14, 2019, Last accessed June 21, 2021, https://pubmed.ncbi.nlm.nih. gov/31728781/.

45 Wikipedia. "Voodoo death." Last accessed June21, 2021, https://en.wikipedia.org/wiki/Voodoo_death.

46 Susan Maas, "Lucky No. 8 (and 972)," Discovery, University of Minnesota, Fall 2020, Last accessed July 27, 2021, https://discoverymag .umn.edu/stories/lucky-no-8-and-972.

47 Lemelson-MIT, "Paul Winchell," Artificial Heart, Healthcare, Last accessed June 21, 2021, https://lemelson.mit.edu/resources/paul-winchell.

48 Sumati Yengkhom, "Kolkata man lives 10 years with artificial heart," *The Times of India*, Updated September 10, 2019, Last accessed July 12, 2021, https://timesofindia.indiatimes.com/city/kolkata/man-lives-10-yrs-with-artificial-heart/articleshow/71057046.cms.

49 Madeleine, "The Bible's Meaning of 'Heart,'" Theology, my lamp blog, December 17, 2017, last accessed July 12, 2021, http://my lampblog.com/the-bibles-meaning-of-heart/.

50 Lindsell, Harold. 1976. *The Battle for the Bible* (Grand Rapids: Zondervan Publishing House).

51 Wikipedia. "Pharisees." Last accessed June 22, 2021, https://en.wiki pedia.org/wiki/Pharisees.

52 Wikipedia. "Hasmonean dynasty." Last accessed July 27, 2021, https:// en. wikipedia.org/wiki/Hasmonean_dynasty.

53 Butterfield, Herbert. 1949. *The Origins of Modern Science* (London: G.Bell and Sons Ltd).

54 Tozer, A. W. 1975. "The Omnipotence of God," in *The Knowledge of the Holy* (New York: First Harper & Row Jubilee edition), 72.

55 Wikipedia. "Ocean liner." Last accessed June 22, 2021, https://en.wiki pedia.org/wiki/Ocean_liner.

56 Wikipedia. "Steamship." Last accessed June 22, 2021, https://en.wiki pedia.org/wiki/Steamship.

57 Wikipedia. "Isambard Kingdom Brunel." Last accessed June 22, 2021, https://en.wikipedia.org/wiki/Isambard_Kingdom_Brunel.

58 Wikipedia, "Steamship," op. cit.

59 Mecholic, "What Are The Advantages of Steam Turbine Over The Steam Engine?" Power Plant Engineering, Thermal Engineering, Last accessed June 22, 2021, https://www.mecholic.com/2018/12/advant ages-of-steam-turbine.html.

60 Wikipedia. "RMS Victorian." Last accessed June 22, 2021, https://en. wikipedia.org/wiki/RMS_Victorian.

61 Wikipedia. "RMS Mauretania (1906)." Last accessed June 22, 2021, https://en.wikipedia.org/wiki/RMS_Mauretania_(1906).

62 Wikipedia. "Olympic-class ocean liner." Last accessed June 22, 2021, https://en.wikipedia.org/wiki/Olympic-class_ocean_liner.

63 Seth Borenstein, "Titanic's legacy: A fascination with disasters," NBC News, March 31, 2012, Last accessed July 12, 2021, https://www. nbcnews.com/id/wbna46916279.

64 Technology.org, "Another ship was watching Titanic go down–why no one helped?" July 23, 2018, Last accessed July 12, 2021, https:// www.technology.org/2018/07/31/ another-ship-was-watching-titanic-go-down-why-no-one-helped/.

65 History.com editors, "Titanic," History, Updated: Apr 9, 2021. https:// www.history.com/topics/early-20th-century-us/titanic.

66 Ruth Ruby, "Titanic: the Hero Musicians," HistorianRuby: An Historian's Miscellany, January 14, 2018, Last accessed July 12, 2021, https://historianruby.com/.

67 Musical America Worldwide, "The Titanic's Musicians: Heroes All," Musical America Blogs, Last accessed June 22, 2021, https://www. musicalamerica.com/mablogs/?page_id=4544.

68 Tony Carnes, "Faith on the Decks of the Titanic," NYC Religions, *NY Times*, April 15, 2021, https://nycreligion. info/2021-faith-on-the-decks-of-the-titanic/.

69 Douglas W.Mize, "As Titanic sank, he pleaded, 'believe in the Lord Jesus!'" News Article, Baptist Press, April 13, 2012, Last accessed June 22, 2021, https://www.baptistpress.com/resource-library/news/ as-titanic-sank-he-pleaded-believe-in-the-lord-jesus/.

70 Ibid.

71 Maragh, Alvin Lloyd. 2006. "The Healing Ministry of Jesus as Recorded in the Synoptic Gospels." Loma Linda University Electronic Theses, Dissertations & Projects, 457. http://scholarsrepository.llu.edu/etd/457.

72 Ibid.

73 Tozer, "The Omnipotence of God," op. cit.

74 Maragh, op. cit.

75 Michael Reeves, "Did You Know That Charles Spurgeon Struggled with Depression?" Crossway, February 24, 2018, Last accessed June 23, 2021, https://www.crossway.org/articles/ did-you-know-that-charles-spurgeon-struggled-with-depression/.

76 Wikipedia. "Charlotte Elliott." Last accessed June 23, 2021, https://en. wikipedia.org/wiki/Charlotte_Elliott.

77 Wikipedia. "Just as I Am (hymn)." Last accessed June 23, 2021, https:// en.wikipedia.org/wiki/Charlotte_Elliott.

78 Wikipedia, "Charlotte Elliott," op. cit.

79 Stephen Flick, "The Christian Founding of Harvard," Christian Heritage Fellowship, September 6, 2020, https://christianheritage fellowship.com/ the-christian-founding-of-harvard/.

80 Wikipedia. "History of Harvard University." Last accessed July 12, 2021, https://en.wikipedia.org/wiki/History_of_Harvard_University.

81 All About History, "History of Harvard," Quoting from: Newcombe, Jerry. 2009. *The Book that Made America Great: How the Bible Formed Our Nation* (Ventura: Nordskog Publishing). https://www.allabout history.org/history-of-harvard.htm.

82 Wikipedia, "History of Harvard University," op. cit.

83 Ibid.

84 Wikipedia. "Charles William Eliot." Last accessed June 23, 2021, https:// en.wikipedia.org/wiki/Charles_William_Eliot.

85 Ibid.

86 Juan V. Esteller, "The Secular Life at Harvard," *The Harvard Crimson*, January 19, 2016, Last accessed June 23, 2021, https://www. thecrimson. com/article/2016/1/19/secular-harvard-esteller/.

87 Wikipedia, "Charles William Eliot," op. cit.

88 Wikipedia. "Golf." Last accessed June 23, 2021, https://en.Wikipedia.org/ wiki/Golf.

89 Wikipedia. "History of Golf." Last accessed June 23, 2021, https://en. wikipedia.org/wiki/History_of_golf.

90 Wikipedia. "Golf ball." Last accessed June 23, 2021, https://en.wiki pedia.org/wiki/Golf_ball.

91 Ibid.

92 Cliff Schrock, "Fifty years ago, Bobby Jones talked about equipment making the game easier and too many golf tournaments on TV," *Golf Digest*, April 2, 2015, Last accessed June 23, 2021, https:// www.golf digest.com/story/fifty-years-ago-bobby-jones-on.

93 Wikipedia. "The Open Championship." Last accessed on June 23, 2021, https://en.wikipedia.org/wiki/The_Open_Championship.

94 Zach Johnson, "PGA Pro Zach Johnson – Golf, Life and Faith," transcript of *Golf Life* interview quoted in College Golf Fellowship, Last accessed March 18, 2021, https://www.collegegolffellowship.com/.

95 Wikipedia. "Zach Johnson." Last accessed June 23, 2021, https://en. wikipedia.org/wiki/Zach_Johnson.

96 The Open, "Zach Johnson at St Andrews," 2015 Video: Putting Perfection, Great Open Rounds, Last accessed June 23, 2021, https:// www.theopen.com/video/ed672c56-9f10-405d-b03c-139657d404d/0_ 6tauq5s6/Zach-Johnson-at-St-Andrews-|-Great-Open-Rounds.

97 Wikipedia, "Zach Johnson," op. cit.

98 PGAtour.com Staff, "Zach Johnson honored with PGA Tour's Payne Stewart Award," PGA Tour, August 12, 2020, https://www.pga tour. com/paynestewartaward/News/2020/08/12/zach-johnson-honored-with pga-tour-s-payne-stewart-award-presented-by-southern-company.html.

99 Doug Ferguson, "Emotional Zach Johnson named 2020 Payne Stewart Award winner," Golf Channel, August 12, 2020, https://www. golfchannel.com/news/emotional-zach-johnson-named-2020-payne stewart-award-winner.

100 Zach Johnson Golf, "Zach's Official Bio," Zach Johnson Official Website, Last accessed August 10, 2021, http://www.zachjohnsongolf.com/ AboutZach.aspx.

101 Godtube, "10 Christian PGA Golfers," Godtube transcript, August 25, 2013, Last accessed July 13, 2021, https://www.godtube. com/news/10-christian-pga-golfers.html.

102 Wikipedia. "Guglielmo Marconi." Last accessed June 23, 2021, https:// en.wikipedia.org/wiki/Guglielmo_Marconi.

103 Finney Media, "History of Christian Radio – Part 1," Last accessed June 24, 2021, https://finneymedia.com /history-radio-1/.

104 Al Seckel, "God's Frequency Is 39.17 MHz: "The Investigation of Peter Popoff," *Science and the Paranormal*, 1987, reprinted in Center for Astrophysics and Space Astronomy – CASA, University of Colorado Boulder, Last accessed June 24, 2021, https://casa.colorado.edu/~d duncan/pseudoscience/PeterPopoff.htm.

105 Wikipedia. "Peter Popoff." Last accessed June 24, 2021, https://en. wikipedia.org/wiki/Peter_Popoff.

106 Mark Oppenheimer, "Peter Popoff, the Born-Again Scoundrel," Culture, GQ, February 27, 2021, https:// www.gq.com/story/peter-popoff-born-again-scoundrel.

107 Wikipedia. "Aramaic." Last accessed June 24, 2021, https://en.wiki pedia. org/wiki/Aramaic.

108 Victoria Emily Jones, "How Measureless (Artful Devotion)," Art & Theology, July 24, 2018, Last accessed July 13, 2021, https://artand theology.org/page/34/?wref=bif.

109 Laura Lieber, "The Piyyut (Poem) Akdamut Milin," The Torah.com, Last accessed June 24, 2021, https://www.thetorah.com/article / akdamut-milin.

110 Wikipedia. "Piyyut." Last accessed June 24, 2021, https://en.wiki pedia. org/wiki/Torah.

111 Hymn Time, "Frederick Martin Lehman," Last accessed June 24, 2021, http://www.hymntime.com/tch/bio/l/e/h/m/lehman_ fm.htm.

112 Nicole, "Hymn History: The Love of God," Nickel-notes Blog, February 14, 2012, Last accessed June 24, 2021, http://nickel-notes.blogspot.com /2012/02/hymn-history-love-of-god.html.

113 Ibid.

114 Graber, Stacie, director. 2013. *Indescribable*. Phoenix: Bridgestone Multimedia Group, Video.

115 Ibid.

116 Voice of Prophesy News editor, "Music of the Message: The Story of 'the Love of God,'" The Voice of Prophecy News, *Ministry Magazine*,

September 1950, Last accessed June 24, 2021, https://www.ministry magazine.org/archive/1950/09/the-story-of-the-love-of-god.

117 Nicole, op. cit.

118 Peter Colón, "The Love of God is Greater Far," Israel My Glory, November/ December 2013, Last accessed June 24, 2021, https://israel myglory.org/article /the-love-of-god-is-greater-far/.

119 Wikipedia. "Pool of Bethesda." Last accessed June 24, 2021, https:// en.wikipedia.org/wiki/Pool_of_Bethesda.

120 Bill Heinrich, "Capernaum: The Paralytic Is Healed," in *Mysteries of the Messiah* (Self-published E-Book, 2016), https://www.mysteriesof themessiah.net/ 2016/01/06-03-09-capernaum-the-paralytic-is-healed/.

121 Eric Lyons, "Controversial Jericho," Alleged Discrepancies, Apologetics Press, Last accessed July 13, 2021, https://www.apolo geticspress.org/ AllegedDiscrepancies.aspx? article=666.

122 Jennie Cohen, "6 Things You May Not know About the Dead Sea Scrolls," History Stories, History, Updated August 29, 2018, Last accessed June 25, 2021, https://www.history.com/ news/6-things-you-may-not-know-about-the-dead-sea-scrolls.

123 Got Questions, "What is the correct translation of Psalm 22:16?" Questions about the Bible, Got Questions Ministries, Last accessed June 25, 2021, https://www.gotquestions.org/Psalm-22-16-lion-pierced. html.

124 Andrew Perrin, "How The Dead Sea Scroll Discovery Changed Christianity," Relevant Magazine, September 5, 2017, Last accessed June 25, 2021, https://www.relevantmagazine.com/current/ how-the-dead-sea-scroll-discovery-changed-christianity/.

125 Biblical Archaeology Society Staff, "The Tel Dan Inscription: The First Historical Reference of King David from the Bible," Biblical Archaeology Society, June 11, 2021, https://www.biblicalarchaeology.org/daily/ biblical-artifacts/the-tel-dan-inscription-the-first-historical-evidence-of-the-king-david-bible-story/.

126 John Noble Wilford, "From Israeli Site, News of House of David," *New York Times*, August 6, 1993, Last accessed June 25, 2021, https:// www. nytimes.com/1993/08/06/world/from-israeli-site-news-of-house-of-david.html.

127 Amy J. Bratcher, "Navigation at Sea, History of," Water Encyclopedia, Last accessed June 25, 2021, http://www.waterencyclopedia.com/Mi-Oc/ Navigation-at-Sea-History-of.html.

128 Danielle Hall, "Currents, Waves, and Tides," Ocean, *Smithsonian*, August 2020, https://ocean.si.edu/planet-ocean/tides-currents/currents -waves-and-tides.

129 Rice University, "Portuguese Nautical Master Charts," Reformed University Fellowship, Rice University, Last accessed June 25, 2021, https://www.ruf.rice.edu/~feegi/maps.html.

130 NOAA, "A History of Charting Our Nation's Waters," NOAA's National Ocean Service, Foundations: Nautical Charts, NOAA, Revised January 21, 2021, Last accessed June 25, 2021, https://celebrating200years.noaa.gov/foundations/nautical _charts/welcome.html.

131 Wikipedia. "Matthew Fontaine Maury." Last accessed June 25, 2021, https://en.wikipedia.org/wiki/Matthew_Fontaine_Maury.

132 Ibid.

133 Ibid.

134 Ibid.

135 Mark Cartwright, "Ancient Greek Medicine," *World History Encyclopedia*, April 11, 2018, Last accessed June 25, 2021, https://www .worldhistory.org/Greek_Medicine/.

136 C. Ben Mitchell, "The Christian Hippocratic Tradition in Medicine," Center for Bioethics & Human Dignity, Trinity International University, November 5, 2010, Last accessed June 25, 2021, https://. cbhd.org/content/christian-hippocratic-tradition-medicine

137 Wikipedia. "Hippocratic Oath." Last accessed June 25, 2021, https://en.wikipedia.org/wiki/Hippocratic_Oath.

138 C. Ben Mitchell, op. cit.

139 Tommy Shultz, "Body Bad, Spirit Good," Diocesan, October 25, 2019, Last accessed October 1, 2021, https://diocesan.com/body-bad-spirit-good/.

140 Ferngren, Gary B. 2016. *Medicine & Health Care in Early Christianity* (Baltimore: Johns Hopkins University Press).

141 Ibid.

142 C. Ben Mitchell, op. cit.

143 Ferngren, op. cit.

144 C. Ben Mitchell, op. cit.

145 Tooley, Michael. 1988. "In Defense of Abortion and Infanticide," in *What Is a Person*, ed. Michael F. Goodman, (Totowa, New Jersey: Humana Press).

146 Roslyn Public Schools [Long Island, NY], "Reasons for European Immigration," Roslyn Public Schools, Last accessed June 25, 2021,

https://www.roslynschools.org/cms/lib/NY02205423/Centricity/Domain/418/Immigration.pdf.

147 Wikipedia. "Decolonization of the Americas." Last accessed August 9, 2021, https://en.wikipedia.org/wiki/Decolonization_of_the_Americas.

148 David Armitage, "The Declaration of Independence in Global Perspective," AP US History Study Guide, The Gilder Lehrman Institute of American History, 2009-2019, Last accessed June 26, 2021, http://ap. gilderlehrman.org/ history-by-era/road-revolution/essays/declaration-independence-global-perspective.

149 History.com editors, "Fourth of July – Independence Day," History, Updated: Jan 8, 2021, https://www.history.com/topics /holidays/july-4th.

150 National Archives, "Declaration of Independence: A Transcription," America's Founding Documents, National Archives, https://www.archives.gov/founding-docs/declaration-transcript.

151 Wikipedia. "Industrial Revolution." Last accessed August 11, 2021, https://en.wikipedia.org/wiki/Industrial_Revolution.

152 Scott Thompson, "Common Jobs During the Industrial Revolution," The Classroom, Updated June 27, 2018, Last accessed August 11, 2021, https:// www.theclassroom.com/common-jobs-during-the-industrial-revolution-12082916.html.

153 Christian History editorial staff, "Fanny Crosby, Prolific and Blind Hymn Writer," at Christianity Today website, Last accessed June 26, 2021, https://www.christianitytoday.com/ history/people/poets/fanny-crosby.html.

154 Wikipedia. "Fanny Crosby." Last accessed June 26, 2021, https://en.wikipedia.org/wiki/Fanny_Crosby.

155 Paperless Hymnal, "Fanny J. Crosby," Last accessed June 26, 2021, http://www.paperlesshymnal.com/tph/stories/fannyjcrosby/index. htm.

156 Wikipedia, "Franny Crosby," op. cit.

157 "Fanny Crosby, Prolific and Blind Hymn Writer," op. cit.

158 Wikipedia, "Fanny Crosby," op. cit.

159 Ibid.

160 Paperless Hymnal, op. cit.

161 Wikipedia. "Fanny Crosby."

162 The Greek Designers, "Drama Masks: Thalia & Melpomene," March 7, 2016, Last accessed June 26, 2021, https://thegreekdesigners.com/2016/03/07/drama-masks-thalia-melpomene/ Copyright 2021. The Greek Designers ® Registered Trademark No: 016623944. Used with permission.

163 History of Greek Theatre, "Masks in Greek Theatre," History of Greek Drama, Last accessed June 26, 2021, https://historyofgreekdrama-rubybourke.weebly.com/masks-in-greek-theatre.html.

164 University of Delaware, "Mystery and Morality Plays," British Literature Wiki, Last accessed June 26, 2021, https://sites.udel.edu/ britlitwiki/ mystery-and-morality-plays/.

165 Paul S. Wingert, "Masks," By courtesy of *Encyclopedia Britannica*, Inc., copyright 2020; used with permission, Last accessed June 26, 2021, https://www.britannica.com/art/mask-face-covering.

166 Ibid.

167 Alyssa Maio, "How The Best Method Actors Prepare For Their Roles," Studio Binder, June 14, 2020, Last accessed June 26, 2021, https://www.studiobinder.com/blog/what-is-method-acting/.

168 Ibid.

169 Wikipedia. "Method acting." Last accessed June 26, 2021, https://en.wikipedia.org/wiki/Method_acting.

170 Wikipedia. "Masking (personality)." Last accessed June 26, 2021, https://en.wikipedia.org/wiki/Masking_(personality).

171 Got Questions, "Why did Moses have to wear a veil?" Last accessed October 1, 2021, https://www.gotquestions.org/Moses-veil.html.

172 Wikipedia. "Metamorphosis." Last accessed June 26, 2021, https://en.wikipedia.org/wiki/Metamorphosis.

173 Ashley Seehorn, "Indirect Development vs. Direct Development," Sciencing, Updated November 22, 2019, Last accessed June 26, 2021, https://sciencing.com/indirect-development-vs-direct-development-8352326.html.

174 Wikipedia, "Metamorphosis," op. cit.

175 American Museum of Natural history, "The Immortal Jellyfish," May 4, 2015, Last accessed June 216, 2021, https://www.amnh.org/explore / news-blogs/on-exhibit-posts/the-immortal-jellyfish.

176 Oxford English Dictionary, "met·a·mor·pho·sis," noun, Google English Dictionary, Last accessed June 26, 2021, https://www.google.com/ search?q=metamorphosis+definition&client=firefox-b-1-d.

177 Deborah Byrd and Eleanor Imster, "What Will Happen When Our Sun Dies?" Space, Earth Sky, May 11, 2018, Last accessed June 26, 2021, https://earthsky.org/ space/what-will-happen-when-our-sun-dies/.

178 Wikipedia. "Big Bang." Last accessed June 26, 2021, https://en. wikipedia.org/wiki/Big_Bang.

179 Ibid.

180 Wikipedia. "History of basketball." Last accessed June 26, 2021, https://en.wikipedia.org/wiki/History_of_basketball.

181 Wikipedia. "NBA high school draftees." Last accessed October 2, 2021, https://en.wikipedia.org/wiki/NBA_high_school_draftees.

182 Wikipedia. "Kansas Jayhawks men's basketball." Last accessed June 27, 2021, https://en.wikipedia.org/wiki/Kansas_Jayhawks_men%27s_basketball.

183 Wikipedia. "List of career achievements by Wilt Chamberlain." Last accessed June 27, 2021, https://en.wikipedia.org/wiki/List_of_career_achievements_by_Wilt_Chamberlain.

184 Wikipedia, "Kansas Jayhawks men's basketball," op. cit.

185 Rains, Rob and Helen Carpenter. 2009. *James Naismith: The Man Who Invented Basketball* (Philadelphia: Temple University Press).

186 Wikipedia. "James Naismith." Last accessed June 27, 2021, https://en.wikipedia.org/wiki/James_Naismith.

187 Wikipedia. "Fred Rogers." Last accessed June 27, 2021, https://en.wikipedia.org/wiki/Fred_Rogers.

188 Rains, op. cit.

189 Wikipedia, "James Naismith," op. cit.

190 Rains, op. cit.

191 Wikipedia, "James Naismith," op. cit.

192 Wikipedia, "Kansas Jayhawks men's basketball," op. cit.

193 Wikipedia. "History of science fiction." Last accessed June 27, 2021, https://en.wikipedia.org/wiki/History_of_science_fiction.

194 Wikipedia. "Extraterrestrial life." Last accessed June 27, 2021, https://en.wikipedia.org/wiki/Extraterrestrial_life.

195 Fontanelle, Bernard le Bovier de. 1686. *Conversations on the Plurality of Worlds* (Reprinted by Berkeley: University of California Press, 1990).

196 NASA Science, "Radio Waves," Tour of the Electromagnetic Spectrum, August 10, 2016, Last accessed June 27, 2021, https://sci ence.nasa.gov/ems/05.

197 Seth Shostak, "Goodbye, Arecibo," SETI Institute, November 20, 2020, Last accessed June 27, 2021, https://www.seti.org/goodbye-arecibo.

198 Wikipedia. "Communication with extraterrestrial intelligence." Last accessed June 28, 2021, https://en.wikipedia.org/wiki /Communication_with_extraterrestrial_intelligence.

199 Elizabeth Howell, "Exoplanets: Worlds Beyond Our Solar System," Space, March 29, 2018, Last accessed June 28, 2021, https://www. space.com/17738-exoplanets.html.

200 Lewis, C.S. 2011. *The Space Trilogy* (New York: Scribner).

201 David Laughlin, "Science Fiction: a Biblical Perspective," Answers in Genesis, August 1, 2001, Last accessed June 28, 2021, https://answers ingenesis.org/culture/science-fiction-a-biblical-perspective/.

202 Wikipedia. "The Star." Last accessed June 28, 2021, *https://en.wiki pedia. org/wiki/The_Star_(Clarke_short_story)*.

203 Wikipedia. "William Whiting Borden." Last accessed June 28, 2021, https://en.wikipedia.org/wiki/William_Whiting_Borden.

204 Southern Nazarene University, "No Reserves. No Retreats. No Regrets," William Borden's Life, Southern Nazarene University, Last accessed June 28, 2021, http://home.snu.edu/~hculbert/regret.htm.

205 Wikipedia, "William Whiting Borden," op. cit.

206 Philip K. Hardin, "NO RETREATS – NO RESERVES – NO REGRETS," Hardin Life Resources, June 16, 2019, Last accessed June 28, 2021, https:// www.hardinlife.com/blog/2019/6/15/no-reserves-no-retreats-no-regrets.

207 The Traveling Team [Southern Nazarene University], "William Borden, Millionaire to Missionary," William Borden, History of Mission, SNU, Last accessed June 28, 2021, http://www.thetraveling team.org/articles/ william-borden.

208 Borden Dairy, "The Story Behind the Name: Borden, an American Heritage Brand," History, Borden Dairy, Last accessed June 28, 2021, https://www.bordendairy.com/press-room/history/.

209 Wikipedia, "William Whiting Borden," op. cit.

210 Southern Nazarene University, "No Reserves. No Retreats. No Regrets," op. cit.

211 Ibid.

212 Ibid.

213 Ibid.

214 Wikipedia, "William Whiting Borden," op. cit.

215 Philip K. Hardin, op. cit.

216 Wikipedia, "William Whiting Borden," op. cit.

217 Dennis Pollack, "William Borden: "No regrets," Spirit of Grace Ministries, Last accessed June 28, 2021, https://www.spiritofgrace .org/ articles/nl_2011/william_borden.html.

218 Wikipedia, "William Whiting Borden," op. cit.

219 Marnie Chesterton, "The oldest living thing on Earth," BBC news, June 14, 2017, Last accessed June 28, 2021, https://www.wallpanel-supplier. com/news/The-oldest-living-thing-on-Earth.html.

220 Wikipedia. "Date palm." Last accessed June 28, 2021, https://en.wiki pedia.org/wiki/Date_palm.

221 Wikipedia. "Tamar (name)." Last accessed June 28, 2021, https://en. wikipedia.org/wiki/Tamar_(name).

222 The Nursery at Ty Ty, "Ancient Bible References to Date Palm Trees Phoenix dactylifera," The Nursery at Ty Ty, Georgia, Last accessed June 28, 2021, https://www.tytyga.com/Ancient-Bible-References-to-Date-Palm-Trees-Phoenix-dactylifera-a/328.htm.

223 Neil Tow, "A Land Flowing With Milk and Honey," Sefaria, Last accessed June 28, 2021, https://www.sefaria.org/sheets/12025?lang=bi.

224 Old Dominion University, "Palm," Bible Plants, Updated April 11, 2007, Last accessed June 28, 2021, https://ww2. odu.edu/ ~lmusselm/plant/bible/palm.php.

225 Sarah Sallon et al, "Origins and Insights into the historic Judean Date palm based on genetic analysis of germinated ancient seeds and morphometric studies," Plant Sciences, Research Article, Science Advances, https://advances.sciencemag.org/content/6/6/eaax0384.

226 The Nursery AT Ty Ty, op. cit.

227 Jim Robidoux, "Palm Sunday: Holy Week and the symbolism of the palm branch," Manchester Ink Link, March 27, 2021, https://manches terinklink.com/palm-sunday-holy-week-symbolism-palm-branch/.

228 Guinness World Records, "Oldest seed germinated," Methuselah, Israel (Jerusalem), 2005, Guinness World Records, Last accessed June 28, 2021, https://www.guinnessworldrecords.com/world-records/oldest-seed-germinated.

229 Nir Hasson, "Ever Tried 2,000-year-old Dates? Now You Can, Thanks to These Israeli Researchers," Haaretz, September 14, 2020, Last accessed June 28, 2021, https://www.haaretz.com/israel-news/.pre mium-2-000-year-old-seeds-produce-ripe-dates-in-israel-s-southern-arava-1.9152766.

230 Sarah Zhang, "After 2,000 Years, These Seeds Have Finally Sprouted," The Atlantic, Updated on February 7, 2020, Last accessed June 28, 2021, https://www.theatlantic.com/science/archive/2020/02/how-to-grow-a-date-tree-from-2000-year-old-seeds/606079/.

231 The Nursery at Ty Ty, op. cit.

232 Merriam-Webster Dictionary, "Definition of cruciverbalist," Last accessed June 28, 2021, https://www.merriam-webster.com/dictionary/cruciverbalist.

233 The Walt Disney Company, "About the Walt Disney Company," Last accessed June 28, 2021, https://the waltdisneycompany.com/about/.

234 Wikipedia. "Anthropomorphism." Last accessed June 28, 2021, https://en.wikipedia.org/wiki/Anthropomorphism.

235 R.C. Sproul, "God's Communicable Attributes," Ligonier Ministries, Last accessed June 28, 2021, https://www.ligonier.org /learn /devotionals/gods-communicable-attributes/.

236 Wikipedia. "Constantine the Great and Christianity." Last accessed June 28, 2021, https://en.wikipedia.org/wiki/Constantine the _Great_and_ Christianity.

237 Wikipedia. "Arianism." Last accessed June 29, 2021, https://en.wiki pedia.org/wiki/Arianism.

238 Wikipedia. "Isaac Newton's occult studies." Last accessed June 29, 2021, https://en.wikipedia.org/wiki/Isaac_Newton%27s_ occult_ studies.

239 Charles E. Hummel, "Newton's Views on Science and Faith," Christian History Institute, 1991, Last accessed July 29, 2021, *Christian History*, https://christianhistoryinstitute.org/magazine/article/newtons-views-on-science-and-faith.

240 Wikipedia, "Isaac Newton's occult studies," op. cit.

241 John H. Lienhard, "Newton and the Mint," No. 2380, Engines of Our Ingenuity, University of Houston, Last accessed June 29, 2021, https://uh.edu/engines/epi2380.htm.

242 Jane Desborough, "Isaac Newton and the Royal Mint," Science Museum UK Blog, January 4, 2020, Last accessed June 29, 2021, https://blog.sciencemuseum.org.uk/isaac-newton-and-the-royal-mint/.

243 Isaac Newton, "Newton's Mint Papers," The Newton Project, Last accessed August 13, 2021, https://www.newtonproject.ox.ac.uk/texts/newtons-works/mint.

244 Wikipedia. "Early life of Isaac Newton." Last accessed August 13, 2021, https://en.wikipedia.org/wiki/Early_life_of_Isaac_Newton.

245 Wikipedia. "Reflecting telescope." Last accessed August 13, 2021, https://en .wikipedia.org/wiki/Reflecting_telescope.

246 Jim Lord, "The Isaac Newton Story," The Character Network, June 11, 2011, Last accessed August 13, 2021, http://thecharacternetwork.org/the-isaac-newton-story/.

247 Wikipedia. "Isaac Newton." Last accessed June 29, 2021, https://en.wikipedia.org/wiki/Isaac_Newton.

248 Robert C. Cowen, "Sir Isaac Newton: Charting the Course of Modern Thought," *Christian Science Monitor*, July 17, 1987, Last accessed June 29, 2021, https://www.csmonitor.com/1987/0717 /znewt.html.

249 Wikipedia, "Isaac Newton," op. cit.

250 The Neonatal Trust, "Famous People Born Prematurely," Last accessed July 14, 2021, https://www.neonatal trust.org.nz/for-parents/famous-prems/famous-people-born-prematurely/.

251 Wikipedia, "Isaac Newton," op. cit.

252 Patricia Fara, "Year of Wonders 1665-1667," National Trust UK, excerpted from Woolsthorpe Manor Guidebook, Last accessed June 30,2021, https://www.nationaltrust.org.uk/woolsthorpe-manor/features/year-of-wonders.

253 Wikipedia. "Shell Mera." Wikipedia, Last accessed June 30, 2021, https://en.wikipedia.org/wiki/Shell_Mera.

254 Wikipedia. "Operation Auca." Last accessed June 30, 2021, https://en.wikipedia.org/wiki/Operation_Auca.

255 Ibid.

256 Kathryn Long and Carolyn Nystrom, "Martyrs to the Spear," *Christianity Today*, Last accessed June 30, 2021, https://www.christian itytoday.com/history/issues/issue-89/martyrs-to-spear.html.

257 Wikipedia. "Dayuma." Last accessed June 30, 2021, https://en.wikipedia.org/wiki/Dayuma.

258 Wheaton College, "What's In a Name?" To Carry the Light Farther, 2016 Wheaton College Exhibit, jointly created by staff members of the Billy Graham Center Archives (Paul Ericksen, Bob Shuster) and Buswell Library's College Archives and Special Collections (David Malone, David Osielski, Keith Call), Last accessed July 14, 2021, https://www2.wheaton.edu/bgc/archives/exhibits/ecuador1956/06%20what%27s%20in%20a%20name.htm.

259 Wikipedia, "Dayuma," op. cit.

260 Marcia Hall, "Marcia Hall Says," Marcia Hall's response to "The Huaorani (Waorani)," The Huaorani Intangible Zone, July 16, 2012, Last accessed June 30, 2021, https://huaoraniintangiblezone.wordpress.co/the-huaorani-waorani/.

261 Judith Kimerling, "Indigenous Peoples and the Oil Frontier in Amazonia: The Case of Ecuador, ChevronTexaco, and Aguinda V. Texaco," New York University Journal of International Law and Politics, November 3, 2006, Last accessed June 30, 2021, https://nyujilp.org/wp-content/uploads/2013/02/38.3-Kimerling.pdf.

262 Rainforest Relief, "Chevron Texaco," Texaco Crude, Ecuador, Petroleum, Rainforest Relief, 2004, Last accessed June 30, 2021, https://www.rainforestrelief.org/What_to_Avoid_and_Alternatives/Petroleum/Ecuador/Texaco_Crude.html.

263 The Huaorani Intangible Zone, "The Huaorani (Waorani)," July 16, 2012, Last accessed June 30, 2021, huaoraniintangiblezone.wordpress .com.

264 Madeline Arthington, "After Jim Elliot—the Good, Bad and the Ugly," International Mission Board (IMB) – Southern Baptist, April 22, 2019, Last accessed June 30, 2021, https://www.imb.org/2019 /04/22/ after-jim-elliot-good-bad-ugly/.

265 Wikipedia, "Operation Auca," op. cit.

266 Beckerman, Stephen et al, "Life histories, blood revenge, and reproductive success among the Waorani of Ecuador," Research Article, *PNAS* [National Academy of Sciences of the United States of America], https:// www.pnas.org/content/106/20/8134.

267 Wikipedia, "Operation Auca," op. cit.

268 "Marcia Hall says," op. cit.

269 Wikipedia. "Nemonte Nenquimo." Last accessed June 30, 2021, https:// en.wikipedia.org/wiki/Nemonte_Nenquimo.

270 Kevin Davis, "For Snakes' Sake," South Florida Sun Sentinel, September 28, 1986, Last accessed June 30, 2021, https://www.sun-sentinel.com/ news/fl-xpm-1986-09-28-8602270572-story.html.

271 Ronen Bergman, "The secret history of Mossad, Israel's feared and respected intelligence agency," Middle East, *New Statesman*, August 15, 2018, Last accessed June 30, 2021, https://www.newstatesman.com/ world/middle-east/2018/08/ secret-history-mossad-israel-s-feared-and-respected-intelligence-agency.

272 Resa Matthews, "How the FBI took down Russian spies living in the U.S. and posing as Americans," CBS NEWS, Updated on: October 14, 2020, Last accessed July 1, 2021, https://www.cbsnews.com/news/ russian-spy-fbi-united-states-operation-ghost-stories/.

273 Wikipedia. "Cambridge Five." Last accessed September 9, 2021, https:// en. wikipedia.org/wiki/Cambridge_Five.

274 Wikipedia. "Mole (espionage)." Last accessed September 9, 2021, https:// en.wikipedia.org/wiki/Mole_(espionage).

275 P. F. Sloan and Steve Barri. 1966. ...And I Know You Wanna Dance, "Secret Agent Man," Track2, #1, Imperial 66159, vinyl LP record.

276 Farlex, the Free Dictionary, "Walk a Tightrope," Farlex, Idioms, Last accessed July 1, 2021, https://idioms.thefreedictionary.com/walk +a+tightrope.

277 Oriana Leckert, "An Abridged History of Funambulists," Stories, Atlas Obscura, November 5, 2014, Last accessed July 1, 2021, https://www. atlasobscura.com/articles/an-abridged-history-of-funambulists.

278 Wikipedia. "Tightrope walking." Last accessed July 1, 2021, https://en.wikipedia.org/wiki/Tightrope_walking.

279 Oriana Leckert, op. cit.

280 Karen Abbott, "The Daredevil of Niagara Falls," *Smithsonian*, October 18, 2011, Last accessed July 1, 2021, https://www.smithsonianmag.com/history/the-daredevil-of-niagara-falls-110492884/.

281 Susan, "An Acrobat, a Wheelbarrow, and a Challenge of Faith," The Charles Blondin Story, Creative Bible Study, Last accessed July 1, 2021, https://www.creativebiblestudy.com/Blondin-story.html.

282 Karen Abbott, op. cit.

283 Oriana Leckert, op. cit.

284 CNN wire staff and CNN's Jason Carroll, "Daredevil completes walk across Niagara Falls," CNN, Updated June 16, 2012, last accessed July 1, 2021, https://www.cnn.com/2012/06/15 /us/niagara-falls-tightrope-nik-wallenda/index.html.

285 Wikipedia. "Nik Wallenda." Last accessed July 1, 2021, https://en.wikipedia.org/wiki/Nik_Wallenda.

286 Ibid.

287 Ibid.

288 Ibid.

289 Kenneth Boa, "How Accurate is the Bible?" Bible.org, April 27, 2006, Last accessed July 1, 2021, https://bible.org/article/how-accurate-bible.

290 Dave Roos, "7 Ways the Printing Press Changed the World," History, Updated: September 3, 2019, Last accessed July 1, 2021, https://www.history.com/news/printing-press-renaissance.

291 Mervyn C. Fry, "Radio's First Voice...Canadian!" *The Cat's Whisker - Official Voice of the Canadian Vintage Wireless Association*, Vol. 3, No. 1, March 1973, Last accessed July 1, 2021, https://www.ieee.ca/millennium/radio/radio_birth.html.

292 Mark Rogers, "Story Behind Broadcasting the Gospel," *Christian History & Biography*, March 2, 2010, in *Christianity Today*, Last accessed July 1, 2021, https://www.christianitytoday.com/history/2010/march / broadcasting-gospel.html.

293 Wikipedia. "Charles E. Fuller." Last accessed July 2, 2021, https://en.wikipedia.org/wiki/Charles_E._Fuller.

294 Philip Goff, ""We Have Heard the Joyful Sound": Charles E. Fuller's Radio Broadcast and the Rise of Modern Evangelicalism," *Religion and American Culture: A Journal of Interpretation*, Vol. 9, No. 1 (Winter, 1999), 67, Published By: University of California Press. Used with

permission of Philip Goff, Executive Director of the Center for the Study of Religion and American Culture, Indiana University–Purdue University Indianapolis.

295 Charles Fuller, Grace Fuller, and Billy Graham, "Charles & Grace Fuller with Billy Graham at LA Crusade - Oct 12, 1949," Fuller Seminary – Hubbard Library, SoundCloud recording, Last accessed July 2, 2021, https://soundcloud.com/user-638024424/ charles-grace-fuller-with-billy-graham-at-la-crusade-oct-12-1949.

296 Ibid.

297 Adam Graham, "Religious Dramas on Radio, Part One," The Great Detectives of Old Time Radio, July 30, 2011, Last accessed July 2, 2021, https://www.greatdetectives.net/detectives/religious-dramas-radio/.

298 Focus on the Family, "Radio Theatre" and "Adventures in Odyssey," Ministries & Shows, Last accessed July 2, 2021, https://www.focuson thefamily.com/about/programs/.

299 Introduction to each "Unshackled" radio drama.

300 April Neill, Unshackled! "[T]he longest running radio drama in history is on a mission to increase their impact with new technologies," EIN NEWSWIRE, Press Releases, February 25, 2019, Last accessed July 2, 2021, https://www.einnews.com/pr_news/477432955/unshackled-the-longest-running-radio-drama-in-history-is-on-a-mission-to-increase-their-impact-with-new-technologies.

301 Wikipedia. "*Unshackled!*" Last accessed July 2, 2021, https://en.wiki pedia.org/wiki/Unshackled!.

302 Pacific Garden Mission, "Unshackled," Our History, Last accessed July 2, 2021, https://unshackled.org/about-us/our-history/.

303 Pacific Garden Mission, "Unshackled! Radio Program," Last accessed July 2, 2021, https://www.pgm.org/who-we-are/news-and-media/ unshackled/.

304 Merriam-Webster, "Culture: noun," Definition of *culture*, Last accessed July 2, 2021, https://www.merriam-webster.com/dictionary /culture webster.com/dictionary/culture.

305 Wikipedia. "Role of Christianity in civilization." Last accessed July 2, 2021, https://en.wikipedia.org/wiki/Role_of_Christianity_in_ civilization.

306 Schaeffer, Francis A. 1970. *Pollution and the Death of Man* (Wheaton: Tyndale House Publishers).

307 Bob Capune, "March 15 It's The 500th Anniversary of Protestantism," Duner's Blog, March 15, 2017, last accessed January 4, 2022, http://

dunersblog.blogspot.com/2017/03/march-16-its-500th-anniversary-of. html.

308 Wikipedia. "Martin Luther." Last accessed July 2, 2021, https://en. wikipedia.org/wiki/Martin_Luther.

309 Ibid.

310 Lucy Proudman, "How Martin Luther gave Germans a language everyone could use," The Local de, October 11, 2019, Last accessed January 7, 2022, https://www.thelocal.de/20191011/ how-luther-gave-germans-a-language-everyone-could-use/.

311 Ibid.

312 Nicholi, Jr., Dr. Armand M. 2002. "Pain: How Can We Resolve the Question of Suffering?" in *The Question of God* (New York: The Free Press), 213-214.

313 Wikipedia. "Alex Honnold." Last accessed August 13, 2021, https:// en.wikipedia.org/wiki/Alex_Honnold.

314 Ibid.

315 Wikipedia. "Fountain of Youth." Last accessed July 3, 2021, https:// en.wikipedia.org/wiki/Fountain_of_Youth.

316 Tom Garlinghouse, "Mummification: The lost art of embalming the dead," Live Science, July 15, 2020, Last accessed July 3, 2021, https:// www.livescience.com/mummification.html.

317 Cindy Krischer Goodman, "Frozen for eternity: Can you really cheat death?" *South Florida Sun Sentinel*, July 27, 2019, Last accessed July 3, 2021, https://www.sun-sentinel.com/health/fl-ne-cryonics-convention-20190726-q537cfzjdrbsfdeo2h7z6ge6ui-story.html.

318 Wikipedia. "Mind uploading." Last accessed July 3, 2021, https://en. wikipedia.org/wiki/Mind_uploading.

319 Wikipedia. "Spiritualism." Last accessed July 3, 2021, https://en.wiki pedia.org/wiki/Spiritualism.

320 Wikipedia. "Lee Strobel." Last accessed July 3, 2021, https://en.wiki pedia.org/wiki/Lee_Strobel.

321 Jason Swindle, "Warrior Judges of the Bible," Swindle Law Group, P.C., August 3, 2014, Last accessed July 3, 2021, https://www. swindlelaw. com/2014/08/warrior-judges-of-the-bible/.

322 Wikipedia. "Evil Empire speech." Last accessed October 8. 2021, https:// en. wikipedia.org/wiki/Evil_Empire_speech.

323 Serge Schmemann, "Billy Graham Starts Second Soviet Tour," *New York Times*, September 10, 1984, Last accessed November 10, 2021, https://

www.nytimes.com/1984/09/10/world/billy-graham-starts-second-soviet-tour.html.

324 Tom Minnery, "Graham in the Soviet Union," *Christianity Today*, June 18, 1982, Last accessed January 15, 2022, https://www.christianity today. com/ct/1982/june-18/graham-in-soviet-union.html.

325 David Jeremiah, "What Does the Bible Say About Modern Russia?" David Jeremiah Blog, Last accessed July 3, 2021, https://david jeremiah. blog/what-does-the-bible-say-about-modern-russia/.

326 United Church of God, "A Staggering Archaelogical Discovery: The Mighty Assyrian Empire Emerges From the Dust," Is the Bible True? Beyond Today, UCG, December 9, 2010, Last accessed July 3, 2021, https://www.ucg.org/bible-study-tools/booklets /is-the-bible-true/a-staggering-archaelogical-discovery-the-mighty-assyrian-empire-emerges-from-the-dust.

327 Wikipedia. "Book of Nahum." Last accessed July 3, 2021, https://en. wikipedia.org/wiki/Book_of_Nahum.

328 Stefan Andrews, "The Greek engineer Ctesibius of Alexandria is credited with inventing the pipe organ in the 3rd century B.C. and improving the clepsydra, the most accurate clock for more than 1,800 years," *The Vintage News*, February 23, 2017, Last accessed July 11, 2021, https:// www.thevintagenews.com/2017/02/23/the-greek-engineer-ctesibius-of-alexandria-is-credited-with-inventing-the-pipe-organ-in-the-3rd-century-b-c-and-improving-the-clepsydra-the-most-accurate-clock-for-more-than-1800-years/.

329 Mixtuur, "Why Is an Organ Used in Churches?" Last accessed July 11, 2021, https://www.mixtuur.com/en/why-is-an-organ-used-in-churches/.

330 Wikipedia. "List of pipe organs." Last accessed July 11, 2021, https:// en.wikipedia.org/wiki/List_of_pipe_organs.

331 His Holiness Benedict XVI, "Blessing of the New Organ," Apostolic Journey of His Holiness Benedict XVI to München, Altötting and Regensburg (SEPTEMBER 9-14, 2006), Speeches, September 13, 2006, Last accessed July 11, 2021, https://www. vatican.va/content/ benedict-xvi/en/speeches/2006/september/ documents/hf_ben-xvi_spe_ 20060913_alte-kapelle-regensburg.html.

332 Biography.com editors, "Johann Sebastian Bach Biography," Biography, July 29, 2020, Last accessed July 11, 2021, https://www.biography.com/ musician/johann-sebastian-bach.

333 Dykstra, Ruth Elaine. 2004. "Johann Sebastian Bach, Tester of Organs," *Possible Orchestral Tendencies in Registering Johann Sebastian Bach's Organ*

Music: An Historical Perspective, Treatise, The University of Texas at Austin, https://repositories.lib.utexas.edu/bitstream/ handle/2152/1123/ dykstrare516726.pdf?sequence=2.

334 David Wood, "J.S. Bach: Orgelbüchlein," Arts & Culture, Indiana Public Media, March 30, 2009, Last accessed July 11, 2021, https://ind ianapublicmedia.org/arts/js-bach-orgelbchlein.php.

335 *BBC Music Magazine*, "Why did Bach go to prison?" Composers, Classical Music, September 14, 2020, Last accessed July 11, 2021, https://www. classical-music.com/composers/ why-did-bach-go-to-prison/.

336 Lumen, "Johann Sebastian Bach," The Baroque Era, Music Appreciation, Last accessed July 12, 2021, https://courses. lumenlearning.com/ atd-epcc-musicappreciation/chapter/johann-sebastian-bach/.

337 Biography.com editors, "Johanne Sebastian Bach Biography," op. cit.

338 Diffen, "Bach vs. Beethoven," Musicians, Diffen, Last accessed July 12, 2021, https://www.diffen.com/difference/Bach_vs_Beethoven.

339 Wikipedia. "Counterpoint (disambiguation)." Last accessed January 15, 2022, https://en.wikipedia.org/wiki/Counterpoint_(disambiguation).

340 Quinta Essentia Quartet, "The Art of Fugue," Last accessed July 15, 2021, https://quintaessentia.com. br/en/#sobre-escrito.

341 ABC Classic Radio, "Best of Bach," June 18, 2019, Last accessed July 15, 2021, https://www.abc.net.au/classic/read-and-watch/music-reads/ best-classical-music-bach/11218082.

342 Michael Marissen, "Johann Sebastian Bach Was More Religious Than You Might Think," Music, *New York Times*, March 30, 2018. https:// www.nytimes. com/2018/03/30/arts/music/bach-religion-music.html.

343 Ibid.

344 Christianity.com, "J. S. Bach: Soli Deo Gloria - To the Glory of God Alone," Last accessed July 15, 2021, https://www.christianity.com/ church/church-history/church-history-for-kids/j-s-bach-soli-deo-gloria-to-the-glory-of-god-alone-11635057.html.

345 Barbara F. McManus, "A Day at the Arena," Arena: Gladiatorial Games, Vroma, Last accessed July 15, 2021, http://vroma.org/vromans/ bmc manus/arena.html.

346 Wikipedia. "Lion." Wikipedia, Last accessed July 15, 2021, https:// en.wiki pedia.org/wiki/Lion.

347 Mysticurious, "Different Symbolic Meanings of a Lion," Last accessed July 15, 2021, https://mysticurious.com/different-symbolic-meanings-of-lion.

348 Dominique Jando, "Tini Berman," Circopedia, Last accessed July 15, 2021, http://www.circopedia.org/Tini_Berman.

349 Wikipedia. "Clyde Beatty." Last accessed July 15, 2021, https:// en.wikipedia. org/wiki/Clyde_Beatty.

350 Elizabeth S. Anderson, "10 Lion Tamers From History Who Flirted With Death," History, Listverse, October 20, 2015, Last accessed July 15, 2021, https://listverse.com/2015/10/20/10-lion-tamers-from-history-who-flirted-with-death/.

351 Wikipedia. "Androcles." Last accessed July 15, 2021, https://en. wikipedia. org/wiki/Androcles.

352 C. S. Lewis, *The Lion, the Witch and the Wardrobe* by CS Lewis © copyright CS Lewis Pte Ltd 1950. Reprinted with permission. (New York: Collier Books, 1970), 75, 76, 180.

353 Ben Stein, "Christ is Savior and Judge of the World," Never Thirsty, Last accessed July 15, 2021, ttps://www.neverthirsty.org/bible-studies/ life-of-christ-ministry-judea/christ-is-savior-and-judge/.

354 Kenya Safari, "True Story of Christian The Lion: Born to be Free," Kenya Travel Guide, Kenya Safari, Last accessed July 16, 2021, https://www. kenya safari.com/christian-the-lion.html.

355 Wikipedia. "Great Pyramid of Giza." Last accessed July 16, 2021, https:// en. wikipedia.org/wiki/Great_Pyramid_of_Giza.

356 Cheops-Pyramide, "Building the Great Pyramid," Franz Löhner's Theory, Last accessed July 16, 2021, https://www.cheops-pyramide. ch/pyramid-building.html.

357 Terrence McCoy, "The surprisingly simple way Egyptians moved massive pyramid stones without modern technology," Morning Mix, *Washington Post*, May 2, 2014, Last accessed July 16, 2021, https:// www.washingtonpost.com/ news/morning-mix/wp/2014/05/ 02/the-surprisingly-simple-way-egyptians-moved-massive-pyramid-stones-without-modern-technology/.

358 Wikipedia, "Great Pyramid of Giza," op. cit.

359 Wikipedia. "Steam power during the Industrial Revolution." Last accessed July 16, 2021, https://en.wikipedia.org/wiki/Steam_power_ during_the_Industrial_Revolution.

360 Wikipedia, "Steam power during the Industrial Revolution," op. cit.

361 Heather Whipps, "How the Steam Engine Changed the World," Live Science, June 16, 2008, Last accessed July 16, 2021, https://www.live science.com/2612-steam-engine-changed-world.html.

362 Wikipedia. "R. G. LeTourneau." Last accessed July 16, 2021, https:// en.wiki pedia.org/wiki/R._G._LeTourneau.

363 Ibid.

364 LeTourneau University, "R. G. LeTourneau," Museum & Archives, Last accessed July 16, 2021, https://www.letu.edu/library/rg-museum. html#Con tentBlock-1-1.

365 Wikipedia, "R. G. LeTourneau," op. cit.

366 KH Plant, "Monster Earth-Moving Equipment," KH Plant Grader Rebuild Center, Last accessed October 10, 2021, https://www.khplant. co.za/blog/ article/monster-earth-moving-equipment.

367 Giants for God, "RG LeTourneau – Earthmoving Innovator," Last accessed July 16, 2021, http://www.giantsforgod.com/rg-letourneau/.

368 Wikipedia, "R. G. LeTourneau," op. cit.

369 Wikipedia. "I Love a Mystery." Last accessed July 21, 2021, https:// en.wiki pedia.org/wiki/I_Love_a_Mystery.

370 Sister Helen Prejean, *Dead Man Walking* (New York: Random House, 1993).

371 Wikipedia. "Helen Prejean." Last accessed October 11, 2021, https://en. wikipedia.org/wiki/Helen_Prejean.

372 Wikipedia. "Charles Colson." Last accessed July 21, 2021, https://en.wiki pedia.org/wiki/Charles_Colson.

373 Corrie ten Boom, Elizabeth Sherrill, & John Sherrill. 1971. *The Hiding Place* (Grand Rapids: Chosen Books, a Division of Baker Publishing Group), 238.

374 Christoph Marty, "Darwin on a Godless Creation: 'It's like confessing to a murder'," *Scientific American*, February 12, 2009, Last accessed July 16, 2021, https://www.scientificamerican.com/article/ charles-darwin-confessions/.

375 Gonzalo Sanchez, "An Extraordinary Experiment," Ends of the Earth, SWOOP, Last accessed July 16, 2021, http://www.ends-of-earth.com/ author/ gonzalo_sanchez/.

376 Christoph Marty, op. cit.

377 Wikipedia. "On the Origin of Species." Last accessed October 12, 2021, https://en.wikipedia.org/wiki/ On_the_Origin_of_Species.

378 Science Meets Faith, "Bishop Frederick Temple on Darwin's Theory of Evolution," Last accessed October 12, 2021, https:// sciencemeetsfaith.wordpress.com/2019/11/30/bishop-frederick-temple-on-darwins-theory-of-evolution/.

379 Gray, Asa. 1861. *Natural Selection not inconsistent with Natural Theology. A free examination of Darwin's treatise on the Origin of Species, and of its American reviewers.* Reprinted from the *Atlantic Monthly* for July, August, and October, 1860. London: Trübner & Co., Boston:

Ticknor and Fields. In Darwin Online, Last updated July 2, 2012, Last accessed August 19, 2021, http://darwin-online.org.uk/content/frameset?pageseq=1&itemID=A567&viewtype=text.

380 Ibid.

381 Adrian M Wyard, "Does Evolution 'do the work of a friend' for the Christian Religion?" Counterbalance, Last accessed January 16, 2022, https://counterbalance.org/evotheo/index-frame.html.

382 Wikipedia. "Young Earth creationism." Last accessed July 16, 2021, https:// en.wikipedia.org/wiki/Young_Earth_creationism.

383 Pete Wilkins, "Charles Darwin on Religion," ISSR Statement, International Society for Science & Religion, January 6th, 2017, Last accessed January 17, 2021, https://www. issr.org.uk/issr-statements/charles-darwin-on-religion/.

384 Wikipedia. "Religious views of Charles Darwin." Last accessed August 19, 2021, https://en.wikipedia.org/wiki/Religious_views_of_Charles_Darwin.

385 Sara Joan Miles, "Charles Darwin and Asa Gray Discuss Teleology and Design," American Scientific Affiliation, September 2001, Last accessed July 17, 2021, https://www.asa3.org/ASA/PSCF/2001/PSCF9-01Miles.html.

386 Wikipedia. "Charles Darwin's education." Last accessed October 12. 2021, https://en.wikipedia.org/wiki/Charles_Darwin%27s_education.

387 Ted Davis, "The Evolution of Darwin's Religious Faith," BioLogos, November 3, 2016, Last accessed July 17, 2021, https://biologos.org/articles/the-evolution-of-darwins-religious-faith/.

388 Budziszewski, J. 1999. *The Revenge of Conscience: Politics and the Fall of Man* (Dallas: Spence Publishing Company).

389 Budziszewski, J. 2003. *What We Can't Not Know: A Guide* (Dallas: Spence Publishing Company).

390 Ibid.

391 Ibid.

392 Wikipedia. "Atlas (mythology)." Last accessed July 17, 2021, https:// en.wiki pedia.org/wiki/Atlas_(mythology).

393 Brett and Kate McKay, "Lessons in Manliness from Charles Atlas," Art of Manliness, September 29, 2011, Last updated: June 2, 2021, https://www.artof manliness.com/articles/lessons-in-manliness-from-charles-atlas/.

394 Brett and Kate McKay, op. cit.

395 Kennetha Gaebler and Timothy Gregory, "Paul Anderson, World's Strongest Man," Unshackled Script, Program #3478, Aired in 2017,

Last accessed August 26, 2021, https://unshackled.org/program/
paul-anderson/.

396 Ibid.

397 Anderson, Paul, Jerry B. Jenkins & James R. Adair. 1975. "Weighlifting
Fever," in *A Greater Strength* (Old Tappan, New Jersey: Fleming H.
Revell).

398 Anderson, "Weightlifting Fever," and "Frustration," op. cit.

399 Kennetha Gaebler, op. cit.

400 Anderson, "'A Wonder of Nature,'" op. cit.

401 Kennetha Gaebler, op. cit.

402 Anderson, "Miracle in Melbourne," op. cit.

403 Kennetha Gaebler, op. cit.

404 Anderson, "Miracle in Melbourne," op. cit.

405 Paul Anderson Youth Home, "PAYH exists to help transform the
lives of troubled young men and their families!" Christ Centered
Youth Program, Last accessed July 17, 2021, https://payh.org/
christ-centered-youth-program-page/.

406 Ibid.

407 Brett & Kate McKay, op. cit.

408 Max Nisen, "This Map Shows How Americans Speak 24 Different
English Dialects," Insider, December 2, 2013, Last accessed July 17, 2021,
https://www.businessinsider.com/dialects-of-american-english-2013-12.

409 Genius, "Let's Call the Whole Thing Off," George and Ira
Gershwin, 1936, Let's Call the Whole Thing Off lyrics © Warner
Chappell Music, Inc, Kobalt Music Publishing Ltd., Downtown
Music Publishing, Raleigh Music Publishing, https://genius.com/
Fred-astaire-lets-call-the-whole-thing-off-lyrics.

410 Ibid.

411 Max Nisen, op. cit.

412 The many examples of regional differences in accents (pronunciations)
and dialects cited in this story largely call for the reader to consult the
ample amount of reference material on the internet and available in other
formats.

413 Wikipedia. "*My Fair Lady*." Last accessed July 17, 2021, https://
en.wikipedia. org/wiki/My_Fair_Lady.

414 Ambra Minoli, "Difference Between Accent and Pronunciation," Sensay,
March 23, 2021, Last accessed January 17, 2022, https://www. oksensay.
com/language-learning/difference-between-accent-and-pronunciation/.

415 Wikipedia. "The Space Trilogy." Last accessed July 17, 2021, https://en.wikipedia.org/wiki/The_Space_Trilogy.

416 Resa Matthews, "How the FBI took down Russian spies living in the U.S. and posing as Americans," CBS NEWS, Updated on: October 14, 2020, Last accessed July 1, 2021, https://www.cbsnews.com/news/russian-spy-fbi-united-states-operation-ghost-stories/.

417 Wikipedia. "Torah." Last accessed July 17, 2021, https://en.wikipedia.org/wiki/Torah.

418 Jewish Virtual Library, "Ancient Jewish History: The Babylonian Jewish Community: (c. Second Temple - 5th century CE)," Last accessed July 17, 2021, https://www.jewishvirtuallibrary.org/the-babylonian-jewish-community.

419 Yedidia Z. Stern, "Conclusion," *Religion, state, and the Jewish identity crisis in Israel* (Washington, D.C.: Center for Middle East Policy at Brookings, Brookings Institution, 2017), 21, https://www.brookings.edu /wp-content/uploads/2017/03/cmep_20170331_jewish-identity-crisis.pdf.

420 Wikipedia. "Judaism." Last accessed July 17, 2021, https://en.wiki pedia.org/wiki/Judaism.

421 Richard Gray, "Microsoft has built a chamber so quiet, you can hear the grind of your bones – and it's helping to fine-tune the next-generation of electronic goods," BBC, May 28, 2017, Last accessed July 18, 2021, https:// www.bbc.com/future/article/20170526-inside-the-quietest-place-on-earth.

422 London South Bank University, "UNILAD beats world record at LSBU," LSBU, November 21, 2016, Last accessed July 18, 2021, https://www.lsbu.ac.uk/ about-us/news/unilad-beats-anechoic-world-record.

423 *Google's English Dictionary*, "vibrant," https://languages.oup.com/google-dictionary-en/.

424 Ethan Siegel Senior Contributor and Starts With A Bang Contributor Group, "What Every Layperson Should Know About String Theory," *Forbes*, November 25, 2016, Last accessed July 18, 2021, https://www.forbes.com/sites/startswithabang/2016/11/25/what-every-layperson-should-know-about-string-theory/?sh=2bdf5ceb5a53.

425 University Corporation for Atmospheric Research (UCAR), "Molecules Vibrate," UCAR Center for Science Education, 2021, https://scied.ucar.edu/ learning-zone/atmosphere/molecular-vibration-modes.

426 Spielberg, Steven. 2011. *The Adventures of Tintin: The Secret of the Unicorn*. Paramount Pictures.

427 Karen Schrock, "Fact or Fiction?: An Opera Singer's Piercing Voice Can Shatter Glass," *Scientific American*, August 23, 2007, Last accessed July 18, 2021, https://www.scientificamerican.com/article/fact-or-fiction-opera-singer-can-shatter-glass/.

428 *Seattle Times* staff, "Tacoma Narrows Bridge history," Local News, *Seattle Times*, Updated July 13, 2007, Last accessed July 18, 2021, https://www.seattle times.com/seattle-news/tacoma-narrows-bridge-history/.

429 Julia Graham, Shayne Love and Sonia Beaulieu, "When Humans Make Structures Shake," *Structure*, November 2018, Last accessed July 18, 2021, https://www. structuremag.org/?p=13852.

430 Controlled Demolition Inc, "Pioneers And Leaders In Explosives Demolition For Over 70 Years," Last accessed July 21, 2021, https://www .controlled-demolition.com/.

431 Joshua 6

432 U.S. Environmental Protection Agency, "Water Facts of Life," Last updated February 23, 2016, Last accessed July 21, 2021, https://www 3.epa.gov/safewater/kids/waterfactsoflife.html.

433 Samuel Taylor Coleridge, "The Rime of the Ancient Mariner (text of 1834)," in Poems and Poets, Poetry Foundation, Last accessed July 21, 2021, https://www.poetryfoundation.org/poems/43997/the-rime-of-the-ancient-mariner-text-of-1834.

434 Wikipedia. "Origin of water on Earth." Last accessed July 18, 2021, https:// en.wikipedia.org/wiki/Origin_of_water_on_Earth.

435 Jim Webster, "Do you think the earth will ever run out of water?" OLogy, American Museum of Natural History, Last accessed July 21, 2021, https://www.amnh.org/explore/ology/earth/ask-a-scientist-about-our-environment/will-earth-run-out-of-water.

436 U.S. Geological Survey, "How much of the Earth's water is stored in glaciers?" Last accessed July 21, 2021, https://www.usgs.gov/faqs/how-much-earths-water-stored-glaciers?qt-news_science_products=0#qt-news_science_products.

437 University Corporation For Atmospheric Research (UCAR), "The Water Cycle," UCAR Center for Science Education, Last accessed July 21, 2021, https://scied.ucar.edu/image/water-cycle.

438 Carnendil, "If the Earth were a smooth spheroid, how deep would the ocean be? Earth Science, Stack Exchange, Last accessed July 21, 2021, https://earthscience.stackexchange.com/questions/7446/if-the-earth-were-a-smooth-spheroid-how-deep-would-the-ocean-be.

439 James Maynard, "Earth found hiding huge reservoirs of water 400 miles below...but not water as we know it," Tech TImes, June 16, 2014, Last accessed July 22, 2021, https://www.techtimes.com/ articles/8553/ 20140616/earth-found-hiding-huge-reservoirs-water-400-miles-below.htm.

440 C.S. Lewis, *The Screwtape Letters* by CS Lewis © copyright CS Lewis Pte Ltd 1942. Reprinted with permission. (NewYork: Macmillan, 1943).

441 Crown of Life Ministries, "Discussion Guide for C.S. Lewis's *The Screwtape Letters*, Lesson 5, Letter 15: Time and Eternity," Last accessed July 22, 2021, https://church.crownoflifemn.org/hp_wordpress/wp-content/uploads/2015/07/Screwtape-Lesson-5.pdf.

442 Serge Schmemann, "The Talk of Moscow; Chernobyl Fallout: Apocalyptic Tale and Fear," World, *New York Times*, July 26, 1986. https://www.nytimes.com/1986/07/26/world/the-talk-of-moscow-chernobyl-fallout-apocalyptic-tale-and-fear.html.

443 Jen Wilkin, "10 Things You Should Know about God's Communicable Attributes," Articles, Crossway, May 15, 2018, Last accessed July 22, 2021, https://www.crossway.org/articles/10-things-you-should-know-about-gods-communicable-attributes/.

444 Wikipedia. "John Newton." Last accessed July 22, 2021, https://en.wikipedia.org/wiki/John_Newton.

445 Caleb Johnson, "Tisquantum ('Squanto')," Mayflower History.com, Last accessed July 22, 2021, http://mayflowerhistory.com/tisquantum.

446 Ibid.

447 Stan Griffin, "The Pilgrims' First Winter In America," Workers For Jesus, Last accessed July 22, 2021, http://www.workersforjesus.com/ f25-12.htm.

448 Caleb Johnson, op. cit.

449 Nathan Dorn, "The Treaty That Saved Plymouth Colony," Law Library, Library of Congress, March 22, 2017, Last accessed July 22, 2021, https://blogs.loc.gov/law/2017/03/the-treaty-that-made-thanksgiving/.

450 Gina Dimuro, "Squanto: The True Story Of The Native American Behind The First Thanksgiving," All That's Interesting (ATI), Updated November 28, 2019, Last accessed July 22, 2021, https://allthatsinteresting.com/Squanto.

451 Ibid.

452 Caleb Johnson, "Voyage of the Mayflower," MayflowerHistory.com, Last accessed July 22, 2021, http://mayflowerhistory.com/voyage.

453 Gina Dimuro, op. cit.

454 Ibid.

455 N.S. Gill, "Who Are the Sun Gods and Goddesses?" ThoughtCo, Updated January 30, 2020, Last accessed July 22, 2021, https://www. thoughtco.com/sun-gods-and-sun-goddesses-121167.

456 Wikipedia. "Astrology and Science." Last accessed July 18, 2021, https:// en.wikipedia.org/wiki/Astrology_and_science.

457 Wikipedia. "Zodiac." Last accessed July 18, 2021, https://en.wikipedia. org/ wiki/Zodiac.

458 Spencer, Duane Edward. 1972. *Mazzaroth* (San Antonio: The Word of Grace), 13.

459 Fleming, Kenneth C. 2012. *God's Voice in the Stars: Zodiac Signs and Bible Truth* (Dubuque, Iowa: ECS [Emmaus Correspondence School] Ministries).

Printed in the United States
by Baker & Taylor Publisher Services